My Jesus Rides A Motorcycle

Adventures In Faith

By Barbara J. Knutson

PRESS

My Jesus Rides A Motorcycle
Adventures In Faith
by Barbara J. Knutson

Printed in the United States of America

ISBN 9781609578688

www.xulonpress.com

Ruth + Leon,

We loved our day fishing — thanks!

Love

Barbara Mandrell

PS 40:5

Table of Contents
of Stories

Introduction

I t is with great joy that this day has come to share stories of my life as a missionary. For twenty six years whenever I tell about these thoughts to friends or groups, I have been told that I should write them down. While I have shared a lot of these themes, many will still be new for even our long term friends. When I first began writing, it was because of the verses of the Bible that tell me to write them down to instruct the next generation regarding God's amazing faithfulness so they will never forget. I knew that if I didn't get the details down for my children that they would not remember. As I've prepared for this, there are details that my children and I don't remember the same and where that has happened I have either chosen to remember through my kids remembrances or skipped the story all together.

When I was young, my family was very adventurous. I learned to not be limited by any boxes in life. As a young mother, I remember hearing quite explicitly from God that I was to eliminate all risky behavior as I now had children who needed a mother. I happily consented to stop riding horses bareback as that was probably my most risky behavior at that time. And that was pretty much true for the next thirty some years of my life.

During the time I home-schooled my children, I used to tell people that we majored on Field Trips. I now realize that was just continuing on my own heritage.

After my youngest child had graduated from college, she was still driving her college car as she attended her next medical program full time and was also working full time. Her college car was no longer dependable so she was sometimes borrowing my car. Even though my husband and I worked in the same office, we found that with different sched-ules we were doing a lot of shuttling. I decided that I would buy a scooter to drive the two and a half mile trip to work.

I called the safety training center to see if they could teach me on a scooter and they said they could. I guess I was trying to avoid learning how to shift gears. The full weekend training arrived and when I got there I learned that their scooter was out of order so I was trained on a motorcycle, which didn't end up being so difficult after all. I have to admit that it wasn't until day two that I learned that besides the hand brake, there was also a foot brake. Yes, attending a training course was a good thing for me.

I knew that I'd like riding all right, but I never imagined that I was going to LOVE this new found skill. My life was about to take on a lot of new adventure and it has become an ever greater adventure with my Lord. I also started to make the connection that after all those years of living carefully while raising my children, the Lord was allowing this new adventuresome skill into my life.

I love the riskier adventures that allow me to see God's hand of blessings, over and over. I hope that in reading these stories that you too can see how clearly our God leads us as we walk with Him in Joy!

One morning we were sitting at the same table with one of our mentors, 90 year old Fred Smith and also with someone that he mentored many years earlier, Zig Ziglar. They challenged us to be a blessing, to ask God each day to allow us to be a blessing. Zig's challenge included to "use the gifts that God has given us to further the Kingdom. Don't be afraid to get out of the boat, be like Peter. Most people don't risk getting out of the boat."

When I went to shake Zig's hand upon leaving the table, he pushed my hand away and said, "No wimpy handshakes," and proceeded to give me a big hug. I like that kind of joy in the Lord!!

Another part of writing this book that I just thought about recently is that if I sell even one book, I will be earning a living for the first time in twenty six years. As missionaries, we give ourselves into the Lords work serving for no charge in whatever way He leads us. This is a delightful NEW thing for me.

This book is dedicated to my father, Robert Daniel Nichols. As a child, one of the things that my daddy taught my siblings and me was that life was for "LIVING." He didn't think it was right to sit in front of the TV set and watch other people living life so he always challenged us to seek our life adventures. We traveled extensively as a family and played together as a family mostly in the out of doors, enjoying God's creation through camping, picnicking, swimming, and all water sports at our cabin. Doesn't everyone know how to light a "one match fire" even if the wood is wet? That is a tradition that I have passed on to our children also. It was his influence that spurred me on to dare to be a missionary, even if he never understood that choice to his dying day. Live Laugh Love was how he lived his life. Thanks Dad.

Acknowledgments

I would like to thank the special people who have helped me pull this book together. My dear friend Julia Martin comes to bat in multiple ways in walking this journey of Faith in the Lord Jesus with me. This time she did the technical parts of preparing the manuscript and also looked up Bible verses. Gina Gray is also a long time friend who is doing a run through of the final draft to check for any other problem areas and is also looking up Bible verses where I've missed some. Another long time friend, Marilyn Davis, is always willing to help where ever needed. For this project she did a great deal of the editing. Eleanor Goodspeed from my choir took a large draft portion home on the spur of the moment from choir to edit. Jeanne Hawkins who is my oldest living friend (93) has spent countless hours over the last two years carefully editing. And of course my dear husband, Dave, played his part so beautifully. His concern was that each and every story would only bring glory to God. He didn't want anything to come off as judgmental or hurtful to anyone involved. He helped me to rewrite a few parts and eliminate others as I agree with his heart to only want to show God's love through the telling of some of our life story. Also I want to thank my children Nicole, Randall, Paul, Ben and Valerie for giving me permission to tell their stories in this book as well. I love you!!

WWJD for Ron?

My family was traveling from Texas to Arizona over spring break with a detour through New Mexico for a family day of skiing. Our destination was my folks winter residence in Phoenix where they are "snow birds" from the cold up North. We were in the outskirts of Tucson seeking a lunch stop. Eventually we exited towards a Burger King.

Randall, my teen-age son was driving. As we were exiting the freeway, we heard a noise under the hood that would need attention. Ordering lunch was first priority and then the boys and their dad went out to take a look under the hood. A man overheard and followed them to take a peek. I understand this is something guys do.

The problem was, as suspected, the alternator had given out. Our kind "helper" gave instructions to a garage that would be fair with us. A local guide was a blessing! Since a new alternator from "across town" had to be delivered, there would be a delay.

I am a person to whom an idle moment is a wasted moment. I needed a project. I straightened out the van. My handsome, loving husband, Dave, has bushy eyebrows which needed trimming and I had my haircutting scissors with me. There in the lot I clipped them.

An elderly, homeless gentleman approached our makeshift "barber shop" and asked, "Lady, how much would you charge me for a haircut?" Stuttering I replied, "Sir, I would be glad to cut your hair." God had decided that Ron needed me. This was a WWJD moment, the wrist bands on my children reminded me. I was blessed to be in the right place at the right time.

I asked how long he wanted it cut. He pointed to Dave and said, "Like his!" We took off about ten inches. His hair appeared to not have been washed for a very long time and I offered to wash it first but he didn't want that.

On his arms were open sores. I thought about Jesus as He touched the lepers. I needed to do like-wise. The cut looked quite good and was almost complete when I noticed the equally long beard that perhaps needed trimming also. This made me nervous. My fear was that I might nip the skin underneath. I pleaded with God not to make me cut the beard. Once again, a WWJD moment. Lord, I am so blessed to have Your help.

Meanwhile, excited workers were eagerly watching to see the transformation in their friend. As I worked, he told me that he picks up the local papers at the café each morning in exchange for his coffee and toast. He panhandles and gets enough money to maintain his lifestyle. People even give him dog food for his dog. He sleeps on a bench in back of the garage and is the gas station's "security." He said, "I have ALL my needs met."

To me that kind of a statement, "I have all I need" is a big opening to point to the greatest gift I know that really meets my needs.

I told Ron, "Really, Ron, I really do have all my needs met, too. I am stranded with my family, I don't know where, but God is with me here to protect me and meet all my needs. I asked Jesus to come into my life and be my Lord and Savior. He leads and guides everything so I'm not ever alone. And, Ron, He loves you as much as He loves me." Now enters the need for patience. Ron is old, I could almost watch his mind clicking slowly. He said nothing for several minutes. The Spirit said, "Wait." I waited. Ron sobbed and sobbed. "Wait." After a few minutes I offered, "You can tell me, Ron, what you're thinking."

He said, people are always yelling at him to clean up his life, saying he needs to go to church, he needs God. He said these are people who are in church every time the door is open. "But," he said, "nobody loves me."

"Well, I do, Ron, and God loves you. If you were the only one on earth, He would have paid the price for your sins to make you right with Him."

Our car was ready so we said, "Goodbye." We visited my parents, The Grand Canyon, Carlsbad Caverns, White Sands National Park and skied in New Mexico on our trip and all of these were wonderful. But by far my favorite hour was the time with my new friend. It reminds me of the most important thing in life to me. "I'd Rather Have Jesus than anything the world can ever give."

Romans 5:8 ASV: But God commendeth his own love toward us, in that, while we were yet sinners, Christ died for us.

Matthew 25:40 ASV: And the King shall answer and say unto them, Verily I say unto you, Inasmuch as ye did it unto one of these my brethren, [even] these least, ye did it unto me.

Motorcycle Whirl

I did a big dance with my motorcycle! I was driving, Dave was riding. We were on a 125 Honda, two big people. We were heading up a steep hill on a small island in the Philippines. The road which had been dirt and gravel was beginning to get paved in cement. The half that we were on was about to jump up onto the new cement that was only done for the middle third of the road. I headed toward the oncoming side of the road to remain on gravel and avoid the six inch jump up to the cement. No cars were coming. Because the hill was so steep, my momentum was slowing in second gear, so I was going to have to downshift into first gear. There was no hand clutch; you just push forward or backward with the foot pedal to change gears. I shifted into first and at the same time as I meant to be decelerating, I accelerated instead. The bike lurched up like a bucking bronco, front tire strait up in the air. Dave had just planted both feet firmly on the ground, (so like him) preparing to get off when he sensed danger. He held on to me and I held on to the bike as it swirled around in a complete 360 in the air! We were quite a show as everyone watched to see when we would crash! I was waiting to crash. However, God had His mighty hand on this and we set back down again right where we started without the bike or us crashing. Better than a Disney ride, although I really don't go looking for this kind of adventure.

If I had let go on one side of the spin, it would have tumbled down the side of the hill. Letting go on the other side would have been worse as there were people around that could have been hit. One of the Filipinos came up and asked if we'd like for him to take the motorcycle up the rest of the way. Yes, thank you!!

"He will give His angels watch over Thee"

We Can't Eat Our Fruit

When we first arrived in the Philippines, we house sat for another family that was returning to the states for three months of furlough. They had a home with a big yard and each Sunday as both security for their home and a way to keep the yard maintained they hired a local man to be on the premises. Local thieves had caught on that the Christians were most likely gone to church on Sunday's.

This man asked us one Sunday if he could pick some fruit from the **Sampaloc (tamarind)** tree. It was a huge tree that grew in the back of the lot and was a fruit that we were not familiar with. It grew a fig like fruit, sort of in the shape of a peanut. We said that it was fine with us. He returned the next day with a friend and several tarps that they laid out under the tree. Then they climbed the tree and shook every last tamarind from that tree. They bagged them, left the leaves and mess behind and left.

Now we were thinking, things mean something different here and we were going to need to ask more questions. At home, if someone asked if they could have some fruit, they may pick a few bags, several if there were lots. But we could not have imagined him shaking every last bit from the tree, likely to sell the fruit at the market. Not wrong, just different than we were used to. I hope the family wasn't too upset when they returned to a barren tree.

We also never once ate from the abundance of our papaya or mango trees.

Even though surrounding the yard was a big wall with broken glass sticking up from the top of cement walls to prevent burglars, they all knew how to get around that. To get into the yard they simply threw a rug over the glass and climbed over. But to get at some fruit, they had a lovely contraption. It was a long stick with a saw at the end. And under the end was a little mesh basket. They could just reach right over the wall and saw the fruit from its tree and it plopped directly into the basket. We watched in amazement.

We decided that if they needed the fruit, we didn't need it that badly and were happy to let it go. We could go to the market and for a quarter buy a papaya or get a whole kilo of mangos for thirty cents. It always hurts to feel the great need some of them have.

Water Tower

I was a happy homemaker. We had four little ones
at the time. Dave was a Senior Bank officer at a
good sized bank in central Minnesota. We lived in
our dream home on a quiet cul-de-sac at the edge
of a park in town. God had filled our home with
lots of opportunities to love people on behalf of the
King of Kings. We were a rest stop for weary people
and overnight lodging for travelling missionaries. I
loved to share the Good News with all who came by
including the man who filled the water softener tank,
the encyclopedia salesman and anyone else who
happened by. At one point in time we were leading
four Bible study groups a week in our home.

One day I was taking our children for a walk. We
had a favorite route that took us over the back fence
of our yard, on a dirt park road, past a water tower to
a street. We'd cross the street and were on a lovely
college campus with nice sidewalks for pushing our
double wide stroller along with the little trail of children behind.

For a couple of weeks I had seen from my living room window across the park that there were painters up on scaffolding painting the water tower. I had thought, "They must be making LOTS of money to do that."

This particular day as I passed by the tower, one of the painters had come down and was taking a smoke break. The Holy Spirit said, "Share the Gospel with him."

In the blink of an eye, I had a dozen excuses why not to do so. He's a man, I'm a woman. What if the kids act up? I won't be able to get a word in with all these kids. What if he rejects the message? Whatever, I ignored that still small voice and walked on. We had a nice stroll through the stately trees on campus, meandered around and visited some friends, then returned home through the front area. I was almost home when an ambulance, siren blaring, passed me. Arriving home, I found that the painter had returned back up but had not fastened his harness properly and had fallen to his death.

God was giving him one more chance to hear the Good News, through me. I had the privilege to share, and had failed Him.

I had some serious talking to do with the Lord. It became clear to me at that moment that if I wanted to be Jesus' disciple and truly follow Him, then I have to obey Him whenever and however He leads me. It took longer for me to forgive myself for this. But eventually I realized that if God forgave me, who was I to continue to hold this against myself? *If we*

confess our sins, he is faithful and righteous to forgive us our sins, and to cleanse us from all unrigh-
teousness. 1John 1:9

From then on, God had my heart. When He had
a job to do that needed me, I wanted to be found
listening and be one that He could count on to obey,
even through hard things that I may not want to do.

God taught me through this experience to take
a RISK. Often when God speaks, the message can
sound crazy to our human nature. If He's asking us
to do something that the world would laugh at, do
we enjoy acting a "fool" for Christ's sake?

I think it is a privilege to be called a fool if that
means a joyful servant of the Lord, Jesus Christ!

*Luke 7:47: Wherefore I say unto thee, Her sins,
which are many, are forgiven; for she loved much:
but to whom little is forgiven, [the same] loveth little*

*Ephesians 5:15-16: Look therefore carefully how
ye walk, not as unwise, but as wise; redeeming the
time, because the days are evil.*

*Luke 22:26: But ye [shall] not [be] so: but he that
is the greater among you, let him become as the
younger; and he that is chief, as he that doth serve.*

Gods Word Poem

God's Word is like a buried treasure map.

Every day I have the privilege of digging deeper,

And laying hold of as much treasure as my
hungry heart can hold.

I may possess freely, for I am

A beloved child of The King!

The Simplicity of the Gospel

W e were living in a small town about a hundred miles away from the Twin Cities in
Minnesota. One of my Great Aunts who I was very
close to when I was growing up was in the hospital and was not doing well. I packed up three
little ones and made the trip to the city to see her.
My mother-in-law was able to watch the children
that afternoon. When I arrived at my Aunt's room,
it was full of people visiting with her. The attempt
at being cheerful really troubled me. People were
saying things like, "You'll be going home soon, and
you'll be able to get back to your craft projects."
Something about that didn't ring true to me, and no
one was addressing the possibility of her going to
her heavenly home.

We spent the night at my in-laws. All that night
I could hardly sleep as I kept praying for my Aunt
Clair. I wondered where her heart was, was she
facing her home-going with peace in her soul. Did
she know that Jesus was her Savior and she was

forgiven and would be welcomed by her heavenly Father? Or was this most important private message something that she may have heard but let slip by? I didn't know we had not talked about that. We didn't talk about that in my family or in my community where I grew up.

That next morning, I just knew that this would be the last opportunity I may have on earth to be sure that the issue of where she was spending eternity was settled and that she was facing her dying in peace. I knew that somehow I had to see her again. But I had a big problem. My mother-in-law had plans for that morning and was not able to watch the kids. So I loaded everyone in the station wagon and started out of town. Going on I realized that I'd be heading right past the hospital. I wondered if it were possible to see her with the kids in tow. I knew there were strict hospital rules about visiting, even more back then than now. I knew that I had to at least try. So I prepped the kids before we went in that we were going to see Aunt Clair, and I don't know if she is dying so we won't talk about that, but we just want to visit a little bit.

I approached the nurse on the floor and asked for permission to see her for a few minutes with kids since she had a private room and would be eager to see the kids. She gave permission. But when we got to her room, there was a cleaning person in that said we'd have to wait in the hall until she was finished. While in the hall, another nurse approached and angrily inquired as to what the kids were doing here. I told her we had permission from the nurse over there, and pointed. As God would have it, the woman who gave us permission was the head nurse! Thank you, Jesus!!

The cleaning was finished and we walked in. Niki was seven, Randall four and Paul two and I was pregnant with Ben. Her room was full of machines and tubes and we had to be careful as we approached her. Randall marched right over the tubes and went directly to her face and said, "You know you're going to die, don't you?" I almost passed out on the spot.

But it opened up the conversation that needed to be addressed quickly as we only had a short time. I asked her if she'd like for me to pray for her. She said, "Yes." I prayed heartily for her and included all I knew of the plan of Salvation and how she could know where she was going if she asked Jesus to be her Savior. When I finished praying she said, "I never learned to pray like that. Everything was in Latin when I grew up. But as I lie here and prepare to die, I just keep looking up and saying, "Jesus, take me with You."

I was elated, and ever since then I have thought over and over of how simple the Gospel message is. We look to Jesus, at whatever level of understanding we have. We trust that He is the Savior who will take us to the Father. *Matthew 18:3 ASV: and said, Verily I say unto you, Except ye turn, and become as little children, ye shall in no wise enter into the kingdom of heaven.* Bless the Lord, oh, my soul!!

Walking Where Jesus Walked

It was the trip of a lifetime; I could hardly believe that it was really happening. I had been so weary in life and ministry. Being away from family and travelling with two friends, I asked to have a room of my own in order to spend as much quiet time as I could with the Lord between outings. I was here where Jesus walked.

We crossed the Sea of Galilee, also known as Lake Kinneret, in a first century type boat like the one Jesus would have travelled in. Relaxing in that peaceful environment, I was able to let my mind start to wander and "have a little talk with Jesus." I was telling Him how tired I was and how refreshing this was. At the same time, I could picture Him during His busy ministry similarly tired and trying to go to the other side of the lake to rest. It was precious; I was feeling as if He were giving me this entire trip to rest from my labors. And because He was weary He understood how I was feeling.

I also could now see that the lake was not so big. I grew up in Minnesota and knew many big lakes so that's what I had always pictured. Looking to the north shore, I could imagine how all the people were able to walk along the shore to get to the other side to get to Jesus. I have multitudes of people that I interact with on a regular basis who need His touch. It is wonderful to be able to minister to them, but sometimes I am really spent. Jesus felt tired, He rested and they caught up with Him again.

While He was crossing over the sea and resting, He was feeling compassion for their needs, they were like "Sheep without a Shepherd." God worked in that moment in my heart to restore my own compassion to do the work that He had given to me in caring for the needs of people. He renewed my vision for the ministry, it was a simple transaction, but very powerful in my heart. His presence and refreshment I still can instantly recall when I remember that time. He promises to be with us always, and His labor is not burdensome. Nevertheless, I needed to be refreshed by Him.

Once we got to the other side, where Jesus had delivered His "Sermon on the Mount," we travelled by bus to Tabgha which is the suggested sight where Jesus made the charcoal fire by the shore and called Peter to visit with Him. When Peter saw that the Lord was there, he ran to Him. Jesus asked him three times, "Do you love Me?" And three times he answered, "Lord, You know that I do." Three times was to equal the three times that Peter had denied his

Lord before the cock crowed. Jesus then told Peter to feed His sheep.

I was still thinking about God's message to me on the lake when He started giving me another powerful message at this site. He was saying to me, as to Peter, Feed My sheep! If I go in His name I will have His strength.

On the return to the bus, I passed a small stand that was selling rocks with little pictures carved into them. I chose one with a fish on it to keep with me to remember this time of re-commission, to "Feed His Sheep."

Matthew 4:19 ASV And he saith unto them, Come ye after me, and I will make you fishers of men.

Sing It To Me

My family has their little joke that goes like this: "If you want mom to remember anything, sing it to her." I can appreciate that as I feel like my brain is often in overload. I remember when I started learning Scripture praise songs. They came back over and over all week long after learning them on Sunday.

Singing is a great way to hide the Word of God in our hearts.

This morning I woke up thinking about a childhood favorite TV show called, "Romper Room." I loved that show and the real fun was at the end when Miss Betty would look into her magic mirror and say, "I see," and then name lots of names and it was a happy day for me when she called Barbie or any of the rest of my siblings.

On my bed in the quiet of this morning I was recalling and singing one of the Romper Room theme songs that goes like this: "I always do what's right, I never do anything wrong. I'm a Romper

Room do-bee, a do-bee all day long." The verses would tell all kinds of good things that good children should do. Like, "Do be a dress yourself, don't be a dress me." "Do be a plate cleaner, don't be a food fussy."

Singing the song that morning, I got to the chorus after the third verse and sang, "I'm a Romper room do-bee a do-bee all day-ay, all day-ay all day-ay all day-ay." My record of the Do-bee song had a scratch at that place, and now fifty years later that's still how I remember it. I told my sister Mari about this and she remembers the scratch also.

Psalms 119:11 ASV: Thy word have I laid up in my heart, That I might not sin against thee.

Philippians 4:8 ASV: Finally, brethren, whatsoever things are true, whatsoever things are honorable, whatsoever things are just, whatsoever things are pure, whatsoever things are lovely, whatsoever things are of good report; if there be any virtue, and if there be any praise, think on these things.

Another Meeting At
A Gas Station

I was staying at a farm in north Texas working on a book. The place was cozy and quiet, the perfect retreat. There was no internet access there so after a few days I decided that it was time to see what was in my email inbox. After driving through a couple of the near by small towns where there was no internet access, I figured that I'd have to drive a half an hour away to a larger town to search for an internet café.

About a mile out of town there was a downpour of rain. Since I was on my motorcycle and I was getting wet and the rain felt like pellets, I decided to back track to the last town. The first gas station was a perfect spot for shelter. There was a woman inside that had ordered her lunch. I said hello to her and because she saw my helmet she began talking to me about my motorcycle. By the time her food came, she brought it over to where I was sitting and we had a chat for an hour. She had been retired for about ten years and although she knew that she was a Christian her whole life, it was only in her retirement years that she started to read her Bible and was getting really excited about her faith. I asked her what church she attended and she said that she wasn't real happy about the church she was going to. They wanted to talk about all kinds of other stuff and she wanted to talk about the Bible.

I had two different speaking engagements the two weeks before this meeting and the message that was the same from both meetings was around the nugget of truth that we are "not to doubt God's love when the trials in life come." That is Satan's favorite tactic, just like in the garden of Eden, our enemy wants to get us to doubt God and His love for us. I told her that. She was so blessed by that little bit that she called me a while later to tell me that she was looking more hopefully now ahead to the future.

Well the rain stopped and I decided to just try to see if there was an internet connection available that I could use to call up my email here instead of having to drive so far. Sure enough, there was access to a local school network that allowed me in. Thank you Lord!!

Two days later when I tried again to access it at this spot, there was a lock on it and I was not able to get on.

When I got home a couple of days later I got a call from her again. She was so excited. She said that she'd been asking the Lord how she was going to get her questions answered and she felt that He had sent me and she was very thankful to Him.

A little side note: When it was time to leave the farm, I went to put my bag into my saddlebag on the motorcycle. First I had to clean out the bird's nest that had been lovingly built during my stay.

Romans 8:38-39 ASV: For I am persuaded, that neither death, nor life, nor angels, nor principalities, nor things present, nor things to come, nor powers, nor height, nor depth, nor any other creature, shall be able to separate us from the love of God, which is in Christ Jesus our Lord.

Precious Bundle

Many times when I see someone, they ask me, "Do you remember me?" Unfortunately, as missionaries and speaking and ministering in many places we often meet and minister to many people and then move on so often times we really don't remember.

My standard answer over the years that I learned was to say, "Please remind me."

One of our churches met some of the needs of the body by having prayer rooms outside of the worship center, staffed by a team of prayer warriors. I loved being involved in this very vital part of the church ministry. Those that were hurting or had any special needs were invited by the pastor before he closed the service to come and get prayed for. We had as many as six rooms going at one time and they were well used. Nothing was off limits that we prayed about with people. Most of the time, it was a one time event. There were a few who came to receive this help regularly. After I pray with someone and commit them and their concerns to God, I usually try to let it go and not carry it beyond that room. I have a mental picture of rolling it off of my shoulders and onto God's, where I believe it belongs.

One Sunday I was walking in the courtyard between services and was approached by a young lady holding a babe of about two months. She asked, "Do you remember me?" I did the usual "remind me." Several months earlier she had come into the prayer room to pray with me. She was scheduled to have an abortion the next morning and she came for prayer, she said that she was giving God one last chance. I prayed for her to have the courage to protect the precious little child inside.

No one had to tell me from the glow on her face now whether or not she was thankful to be mothering this precious bundle! Oh, how I wish we were even more able and available to pray with one another to help each other get through the hurdles in life. Every life is precious to our Lord, Jesus.

Eccelsiates 4:9-10: Two are better than one, because they have a good reward for their labor. For if they fall, the one will lift up his fellow; but woe to him that is alone when he falleth, and hath not another to lift him up.

God's Bike

I was at a ladies meeting and heard another woman say, "we have a missionary coming, I guess I need to host him." I quickly spoke up, "I'd love to be the one to host the missionary." She was glad to "let" me do so.

I didn't have nearly as comfortable of a home as she had and my guest room was a roll away bed in the children's play room so instead of beautiful paintings on the wall, we had wall to wall toy shelves for him to look at. Our simple and modest home was eager to welcome him as he ministered to our church family for a week.

Many people found their way to our house that week that didn't usually show up. They all wanted to talk with the missionary about something and many didn't even know he was there but were drawn there. An elderly neighbor man came by to visit and the missionary said to him, "You're an old man. If you were to die tonight, do you know where you'd go?" That was the first time I'd seen this kind of public communicating of the Gospel message. We had been talking to our neighbor about his need for Jesus, but surely not that directly. We asked the missionary later, how he was able to be so bold? And he stated that he would not see the man again, and this may be his only chance to hear the Good News. Whereas, we were his neighbors and would want to build a relationship. The man's son also came by to bring us a duck that he had shot and the missionary invited him to hear the Good News also.

That made a huge impression on us that it was possible to ask someone about whether or not they knew Jesus. The missionary told us about "The Pineapple Story" which is a book that he wrote about some challenges he faced on the mission field. He talked about those things that got in the way of our being totally available for God to use us in whatever way He wants to. Sometimes we want things too badly and hold on too tight to things that we need to let go of. He told about how the New Guineans kept stealing his pineapples and how angry it made him. He eventually had to give up to God his "right" to ever eat another pineapple. It was in the giving up and being willing to trust God to receive or not receive pineapples according to His will that finally freed him from getting angry at those who stole his pineapples. They were now stealing from God, and that changed things considerably for all of them. It was a story about being freed up to serve God and let Him use you and do whatever he wanted and not keep trying to do things the "human" way that makes sense to us. Many people were really challenged by his stories and we were becoming more sold out to God and His purposes for our lives.

While he stayed with us, he asked if we had a car that he could borrow to go into town. Dave had taken our only car to work. I did have a bike, however, and offered that to him. He was glad for that and asked for a lock. But I did not own a lock. So then he was hesitant to ride it and risk getting it stolen. But based on what he had been teaching us, I decided that I would trust my bike to God and not worry about it and allow the missionary to use it. He really didn't want to take the chance of it getting stolen. So I told him, "All right. I now give my bike to God. He may use it how ever He wants to and if something happens to it, I will accept it as God's will and hold no liability to the man." He consented and left for town without incident.

A few years later, we lived in another town. We had a few more children by then and Dave and I both had baby seats on the back of our bikes, and the older children were getting old enough to ride along on their bikes. In the middle of winter, one day I went out back to discover that my bike had been stolen out of the garage.

A few months later, it was getting close to spring and time for us to ride again. I reminded the Lord about this and reminded Him that His bike was stolen and I thought we may need it for the family to ride together. One day I was passing by a window to the back yard and saw a man walking along the neighbors back sidewalk that was rarely used. He was looking over at our yard/garage area, and my gut was telling me that it looked like he was casing our place. I let my face be seen in the window so that he knew I saw him. Sure enough, he took off out the alley way. I thought, how strange.

A few days later, I got a call from the police department, telling me that my stolen bike had been found a few blocks from our house, parked in the bike rack at the library. It had a flat tire, so the thief parked it and he knew right where he could "borrow" another one just like it. But, God allowed me to see him and stop the event. In the end, I actually got God's bike back. It had been well used that winter. We figured, he obviously needed it more than I did at that time. How nice of God to return it in time for the family bike rides. A few replacement parts and we were up and running again.

James 1:17 ASV: Every good gift and every perfect gift is from above, coming down from the Father of lights, with whom can be no variation, neither shadow that is cast by turning.

1 Thessalonians 5:18 ASV: in everything give thanks: for this is the will of God in Christ Jesus to you-ward.

Proverbs 3:5-6 ASV: Trust in Jehovah with all thy heart, And lean not upon thine own understanding:

In all thy ways acknowledge him, And he will direct thy paths.

Smelly Fish

I grew up being told that I was a "True American," a melting pot of ethnic mix. It took many years to finally find out at least an idea of "what" that mix was. When I married I knew that I was marrying into a one hundred percent fully Norwegian family.

My children are half Norwegian and the other half melting pot. My first Christmas as a new bride my mother-in-law invited me over for a day in the kitchen to do what "all good Norwegians do at Christmas time." We were going to make Lefse and she bought me my own lefse stick which has made the cuts through the dispersing of all of our earthly goods several times over the years.

She was a pro and showed me all the details of how the dough was to be just so. Keep them cold and only pull a few at a time out of the refrigerator and here's how to roll them just right. Here's how to manage my stick for the manipulation of the lefse on and off the grill. Then they had to be placed into a towel and rotated every once in a while.

It was fun and I always love learning new things. Dave and I have kept up this tradition through the years and our family has learned to love and expect their Christmas lefse. Also as we are now away from Minnesota and living in the South, there are many "snowbirds" from the Scandinavian North country that are delighted when we come by with their ration each Christmas. Our list gets longer and longer each year.

We have a sister organization of mostly retired folks called WA's, (Wycliffe Associates) who come each winter to Dallas to volunteer their skills at our mission. Each winter they host a fund raiser auction for a special need somewhere in the world of Wycliffe. Last February was the first time we attended. One of my friends asked me if I'd make some lefse for the auction, something I wouldn't have thought of. I said I would. The Monday of the week of the auction, I woke up thinking, "If they are excited about lefse, maybe someone would be excited about the traditional fish of the Scandinavians called "lutefisk." I called the woman in charge and told her to make up a certificate for a "Lutefisk dinner for four" for the auction. Then I left town and arrived home late Thursday night and the auction was Friday so I had no time to work on the idea, I just sent off the information for the gift certificate.

There were four couples who really wanted it, imagine that!! Smelly fish! And can you imagine that someone paid $350 for a dinner of smelly fish for four! They did!! He was an old man who remembered having some fifty years earlier and had a good memory of that.

On Saturday morning we called our regular supplier of our family Christmas lutefisk. It's so nice to have a Scandinavian store close to home in Plano, Texas called "The Wooden Spoon." Dave called to ask if they had some lutefisk in the freezer. The owner said, "No, we only get lutefisk in at Christmas time." Oh, oh. What have we gotten ourselves into? With the internet, we could find some. There was a supplier in Florida that would ship some to us for $95 shipping. This smelly fish was really going to be expensive. Most other places don't sell except wholesale. Dave decided to call our dear woman friend at the Wooden Spoon again and he explained to her what we had done. She was happy to order some for us!!

As we've gotten to know her over the years, it seems that those of us who are carrying on the home country traditions are becoming fewer and fewer so she was happy to help keep this going. We were sure thankful. She is a part of the group "Sons of Norway" so we joined that group through her and enjoy that fun fellowship immensely. I feel as if God is good at rescuing me from the jams I get myself into!!

Yes, our two daughters and some of our sons and our two daughter-in-laws also have learned how to make lefse. This Christmas we made perhaps 200 lefse. Dave has the feel for the dough and Valerie took over the rolling as she wanted it to be more "perfect" than I make it, really round and really thin, about the best lefse you can ever find! Ah, the tradition is now passed on.

Proverbs 16:9 ASV: A man's heart deviseth his way; But Jehovah directeth his steps.

Love One Another

We had the privilege of doing an "experiment." After a few months of communicating about a certain ministry option, God made clear the place that He wanted us to go for a season. All those involved in making the decision were very much aware that God had matched our skills with a definite need. We arrived at a small island in the central Philippines for a six-week stint with a translator who was translating the Word of God into the local language.

We were all excited about the time that we would spend together although none of us were absolutely clear about what was meant to be accomplished, we only knew that God had clearly led us to this point.

For us, we were venturing into a new area of ministry. After eighteen years back in stateside roles in missions, God was sending us back to the foreign field. Our mission leaders told us where the newest challenges were.

The day that we arrived on the island, we enjoyed getting to know our translator friend. We had known her name from working in the Philippines before, but didn't really know her. We started out on this journey together by having some serious prayer time together. I remember holding hands around her dining room table and asking the Lord to accomplish His purposes for our time together. We also asked Him to make us "one in Christ" and to love one another in such a way that the surrounding community would experience the love that God has for them through witnessing our love for each other. We recognized that all three of us had strong personalities and the potential for conflicts was surely there. But if God wanted us one in Christ, surely there must be a way.

We enjoyed day by day fellowship together and praying for God's will to be accomplished. There were only a few times that we bumped heads a little bit and we made the choice to put on love instead of demanding our own ways. There was one night that we reached an impasse and couldn't reach an agreement. We decided to keep the peace and only pray and not argue. Later that night we had a simple and cordial visit without mentioning the incident. The next morning she asked what it was that we wanted from her? We were surprised because we had given it up completely. We told her and she took care of it. I asked her what changed her mind. She said that there was something about what we said or did in the later meeting that convinced her we were not pressuring her. And, the amazing thing is that project was probably one of the things that God used the most during our time there. Love wins out!

Daily we experienced God's clear leading and miracle on top of miracle as we met with individuals throughout the community. We shared the Word of God with them in their own heart language and they were very eager for this and wanted much more. We witnessed God do many miracles in timing, with whom we met, we saw individuals accepting Christ and people learning how to lead others to faith in Christ. We even witnessed a healing, and there was so much more. When His body truly loves one another, there is a great witness.

We do know that the translator was now convinced that her community was eager for the coming of the Word and was now enthused to help her carry on her work.

I can't know this for sure, but my gut feeling is that the reason that we experienced so much of God's power had something to do with the choice to stay "one in Christ" no matter what the challenges we faced. He wants us "One" and wouldn't He do all in His power to accomplish His work through us when we are "One?"

There is power in the witness of very different people loving each other. It is impossible, and points to an impossible God who allows us to love each through our greatest differences if we choose to Love One Another rather than just ourselves.

I think people want to know that we love them much more than our agenda.

Romans 15:5-6 ASV: Now the God of patience and of comfort grant you to be of the same mind one with another according to Christ Jesus: that with one accord ye may with one mouth glorify the God and Father of our Lord Jesus Christ.

Full circle

We returned to International Falls for a week in the summer just after returning from our first term as missionaries. We had a real happy reunion with these very special people. These are the saints who prayed that God would raise up laborers from the highways and byways of life to serve Him. Then He answered their prayers and called us to get connected at the church and grow up in our faith.

We started our early years as a married couple on the tennis court on Sunday mornings. Our two-year old daughter, Nicole, went on the Sunday school bus with the neighbor kids to church. A very sweet older saint, Myrtle DeRaad, accompanied her to her class and then back to the bus. We rushed off to play tennis and when we saw the bus coming we raced back home just two blocks away to meet Nicole.

Her Sunday school teacher paid a friendly visit and invited us to church. That was the beginning of a new season of growth in our relationship with our Lord. How we thank the Lord for those faithful servants who ran those ministries for so many years. We cannot be the only ones who are the fruit from their labors. But that's where our family began our walk with Christ.

We were excited to be sharing with this special church group about our time on the mission field. One of our dear friends said that there was no one to teach the little kids class that day. Nicole volunteered and we later realized that this was the very class-room that she had attended those many years before and now she was back teaching the next generation. We made the complete circle! God is awesome.

Galatians 6:9 ASV: And let us not be weary in well-doing: for in due season we shall reap, if we faint not.

Blueberries By Motorcycle

We were staying in the Guest House in Manila and regularly visiting with some of our colleagues who were up from our southern translation center. There were many people coming and going so we talked on a first name basis. After a week of regular visits, we were telling some about our son Randall's motorcycle adventure across Sumatra in Indonesia. He travelled from South to North twenty-two hundred kilometers. This involved ferrying his bike a couple of times and travelling through areas all alone for days on end for two weeks. Also there were no roads in some places at the time because the Tsunami had wiped them out.

He had to figure out where the roads would have been. It's a really exciting tale that I'll tell another time. We finished telling this story to our dinner table companions and they said, at least he was riding his motorcycle like this for a valuable purpose. Our son took a motorcycle trip from Oregon to Maine to pick blueberries!!

We asked, "Is your son, Alex?" Why yes, how did you know? How many people do you know that would have driven from Oregon to Maine to pick blueberries and we knew a young man that had been in our Bible study for a couple of years who moved to Portland and then did this. Sure enough, there on the other side of the world, when we least expected it, we got to meet his parents!!

Having to Yield our Fears to God

W hen we were first called to be missionaries my immediate reaction was, "What about the children's schooling?" We had four children at that time, another daughter would yet join them. My perception was that all missionaries live in huts in the middle of the jungle. For some reason I had the idea that all missionaries sent their children off to boarding school. That issue was one that I needed to wrestle with the Lord over. How could He bless us with all these beautiful children and then ask us to send them away for someone else to raise? I've always longed to have the privilege of being a mother and love my children. I considered that perhaps homeschooling would be an option but thought of that as one that I did not feel adequately qualified for. The bottom line, though, was that no matter what, if I was to obey God's call on our lives to be missionaries, then I would have to surrender that which was most precious to me to His loving care and be obedient no matter what the cost.

That was very hard at first, but somehow I knew that God had a wonderful plan for us and whatever situation we found ourselves in that He was able to be the best caregiver possible. I became "willing" to send them off to boarding school if that was required. And then I had peace! Lots of Peace!! God just wanted me to be willing. It wasn't much longer before we were into the training stages for missionary service. God showed me very soon that the position my husband would have as an accountant would most likely keep us in a central location where there would also be schools. My first fear issue was settled!

Isaiah 41:10 ASV: Fear thou not, for I am with thee; be not dismayed, for I am thy God; I will strengthen thee; yea, I will help thee; yea, I will uphold thee with the right hand of my righteousness.

Proverbs 3:5-6 ASV: Trust in Jehovah with all thy heart, And lean not upon thine own understanding: In all thy ways acknowledge him, And he will direct thy paths.

Uncle Rudy

When Paul was a preschooler, we lived in a Wycliffe community across from our International Linguistics Center. Early morning before the rest of the family awoke Paul would join his friend, "Uncle Rudy" in his garden and "help" him.

Once we returned from our years in the Philippines, Rudy had become weaker from an injury to his back but still could be seen out in his garden occasionally or on his short walks with his wife around the neighborhood.

At dinner time one day, we heard an ambulance come through our little neighborhood so we joined the neighbors to go outside to see who it was for. Rudy had had a stroke and they were bringing him out on a stretcher. I drove his wife to the emergency room and waited with them through the night while they did all the preliminary work. This was just before Thanksgiving time so we were kept busy at home with our festivities with the family so we didn't get back to the hospital. On Friday Paul insisted that it was time to go see his friend, Rudy. He had developed pneumonia by then and was not improving. Some of the other neighbors who saw Rudy suggested that Paul should not come but would be better to remember his friend from the last time he saw him. They were concerned that this would be too traumatic for Paul but by Saturday he insisted that he wanted to see Uncle Rudy while he was still alive and not in his casket.

On the way to the hospital, I prayed for Paul that God would comfort him through any difficult reactions. We prayed that Paul would be a "blessing" to Uncle Rudy. When we got to his room, Rudy was in there alone. He was breathing very hard and his tongue had gotten stiff from not being able to salivate for some time. I said, "Oh, dear Rudy, you're ready to go be with Jesus, aren't you?" I took his hand and said, "Let's pray." "Dear Lord Jesus, You have been Rudy's strength in his life, now we trust You to be his strength in his home going."

I felt led to sing the song, "Sing The Wondrous Love of Jesus" to him. I thought that if he was ready to go to meet his maker, what a better way than to go out in a song. I asked Paul if he knew that song, which he didn't. Since we had prayed that Paul would be a blessing, I thought that we needed to sing a song that he knew also. At this time he was ten years old and knows lots of songs, but under the circumstances, all we could think of to sing was, "Jesus loves me this I know." So there in this dear old saints hospital room we belted out the old favorite, the simplest testimony of all. While we were singing, his breath did slow some as he relaxed. Paul said, "I love you, Uncle Rudy. God bless you" We left.

We arrived at the bottom of the elevator and there was his wife and son, ready to go back up after their lunch. We stayed to visit with them just a couple of minutes and then we left and they headed to Rudy's room. When they got there, he was gone. Later we discovered that we had the privilege of being his last visitors, apparently we had seen him take his last breath.

At Rudy's memorial service, friends were given the opportunity to share something about Rudy's life and the impact his life had been. His important friends from Dallas Theological Seminary where he taught shared. Rudy had a role in the leadership team that found the donor for the property our ILC center is located in Dallas so other mission leaders were there. My heart was pounding but I felt that it was important to share something with this group. That even in his old age, he was still having an impact on young people. He was planting a lot more in his garden than flower seeds. He was investing his love for Jesus into Paul's heart. He wasn't too important to be involved with the little children. I think that God liked that. We are thankful for Rudy's gift to our son. Enjoy the choir, Rudy. His wife gave Paul one of Rudy's Bibles. And that is a treasure.

Matthew 25:40 ASV: And the King shall answer and say unto them, Verily I say unto you, Inasmuch as ye did it unto one of these my brethren, even these least, ye did it unto me.

Matthew 18:5 ASV: And whoso shall receive one such little child in my name receiveth me.

The $2 Faith Lady

W e'd been with Wycliffe for twenty-two years. Our mission had sent us out to continue to "raise support." That has been the hardest thing we've ever had to do in our lives.

God called us out of banking to use Dave's CPA skills in Bible Translation. We had and "Isle of Patmos" like experience so that over the years whenever it got hard, we knew beyond a shadow of a doubt that God had called us to this work and He would be faithful to us in every way we needed. Everyone has their area of testing and we are no exception. Neither are we to try to walk in another's "moccasins".

Year after year there was a struggle to pay the bills and a pleading for God to "help" us.

We were at a crossroads and were either going to be successful this time, or need to leave our ministry for a paying job. We didn't have an "exciting" ministry so it added to the challenge for people to see how the accounting on the home front aspect of missions was also vital. There were a couple of our supporters that came along side us in extraordinary ways to help us make connections to gain new support and we are eternally grateful for that.

One was a woman who we've known and loved from the time we first came to Dallas. We were visiting with her and sharing again our woes. She gave both Dave and I each a $2.00 bill. She said this is seed money, and we'll wait and see how God will multiply it to meet your needs. And she followed up to see if her church would be willing to help support our ministry. They were and we had a wonderful visit there with the whole church body who have been very supportive of our ministry.

That was two years ago. We have now just had one full year of adequate support!! I was talking with her and told her that both of us still carry those $2 bills in our wallets as her seed money and are amazed at what God has done. Our support never makes sense on paper, or can it be counted on each month. But in the end, it balanced out to where we had the full support quota that the mission requires for the whole year.

She was very encouraged to hear that. Then she told me of her recent trip to California to visit with her daughter and son-in-law. He took her over to a vase that he had in the living room. She had given a $2.00 bill to each of the parents and her seven grandchildren a few years back. He told her that they could have all spent them, but he decided to put them in the vase and be reminded of how God would be providing for their every need. That also blessed her. So I told her that she was gifted by God as the $2.00 faith lady. And I am very thankful for the $2.00 faith lady. She has held our hands and prayed for us through thick and thin as we've watched for God to do the miracles it takes to stay in the ministry.

2 Corinthians 5:7 ASV: for we walk by faith, not by sight;

Philippians 1:6 ASV: being confident of this very thing, that he who began a good work in you will perfect it until the day of Jesus Christ:

Sky Dive

Dave had a great way of telling people that we were traveling to see our daughter, Nicole. He said, "If I told you she lived in Chicago, you'd have one reaction, but if I told you she lived in Hawaii, you'd have another." Well, she lives on the Isle of Kauai. And God had blessed us with one free air ticket so we had the blessing of going for a visit and also talked our son, Paul and daughter-in-love, Rachel into joining us before their firstborn was to arrive a few months later. We had a lovely time in every way. On our third day, Nicole said, "Today we are going to go jump off of a waterfall!" And I'm thinking, "Yah, sure, you betcha." We'll see!!

We hiked through a maze of some growth and came out to a volcanic outcropping that led to the falls. Niki said that it was a 35 foot waterfall. As soon as she said that, I remembered a conversation I had with my boss just the week before. I told him that some day (far down the road- before I die) I was going to sky dive. He described how they train the troops in the Army to prepare to do this. There is a platform set at 34 feet and some rigging that keeps you from hitting the ground and they practice doing that several times and by the wisdom of the military minds they have it figured out if you can jump at 34 feet, you can jump from a plane.

So here in front of me, God was giving me an opportunity to practice that which I "think" I'd like to do someday. I know the reality of actually doing so was yet to be determined, could I really step out of a plane into thin air? So I had to conquer this waterfall or I could forget that dream all together. I never would have made that connection if my boss had not said that about the army.

There is a volcanic pinnacle that people stand on to prepare for take off. I worked my way over to it, and just knew in my gut I HAD to do this. It was scary, and yet, what did I have to loose? I had my little talk with Jesus and heard the little words, "just jump!" So I did!! Waterfall, here I come, feet first, of course.

You go way down deep into the water, but at that speed you also pop right back up. The real challenge was to swim through the pummeling water to the side to get back up. With elation I climbed back up and determined that even though I had done so, unless I did this a second time I couldn't be sure that I really would step out of a plane. The second time was just as scary as the first. I stood there shaking but finally just jumped. Now I was convinced that I could sky dive and my heart was full of Joy!! For the next couple of days I just kept thinking, wow, I really did it, now I know I can sky dive! Yeah!!

Then I got to thinking, hey, wait a minute. Why would I wait until I'm back in Dallas to sky dive, I had already checked out "Skydive Dallas." (My friend Julia reminded me since why I would wait, cause she and others wanted to be there- sorry, Julia!) (And Randall, who wanted to jump also – ok, I'll go again??) I called and made arrangements and two days later was going through the process. My kids and Dave were worried about my back and had their concerns, but when you want to do something for as many years as I had, this was one dream to make a reality. The people were professional. There were two of us ladies going up each of us with a tandem, experienced person attached to us. The four of us divers and the pilot took off. While I thought it would be scary to jump out, the Lord had gone ahead of me to take care of that. The plane was loaded with duck tape! No kidding. They were flying around pointing out the beautiful scenery and I was just thinking, please hurry up and let me get out of this.

Then the moment arrived, I leaped into a cloud and free fell for the next minute or so from 10,000 feet. That was exhilarating! Here I was traveling at 120 MPH but didn't feel anything but a gentle float. People asked about the wind in my face, but I didn't feel any pressure. The next thing I remember was the "THWACK" sound of the chute opening. I was then thankful that I had a tandem instructor, as I was so enjoying the free fall that I wondered if I would have remembered to pull the chute. I suppose had I known it was my responsibility to do so I would have, but this way I didn't have to worry about it.

He handed me the cords and showed me how to pull them to fly around the beautiful valley. Oh, that was so breathtaking!! For about 15 minutes I maneuvered us back and forth and then handed the reigns back to the instructor. He brought us in for a two feet on the ground gentle landing in a field met by a man on the ground that grabbed the ropes and kept us from even any bounce. There was NO pain involved at all. The only pain was the fear of doing so, and now that is history!!

A while later I was reviewing notes from a leadership conference I had attended in December, one month earlier. One of the exercises was to think ahead the next fifteen years and ask, "What do I see myself doing, etc." One page was the dream page, "before I die I hope to….." When I looked at that again, I saw that I had written, sky dive. I didn't even think I was anywhere near to doing so, but God led me!

Psalms 37:4 ASV: Delight thyself also in Jehovah; And he will give thee the desires of thy heart.

Shipibo Pot Of Great Price

My husband and I spent the summer in Peru with a group of college students who were considering a long term career as missionaries with Wycliffe Bible Translators. Dave is a CPA and was the Chief Accountant for our International Administration for the mission. Three of the college students were accounting majors and they were to conduct an audit of the Peru branch as part of their learning experience.

While travelling in the country with these folks, we were up and down the Andes Mountains as we went to various assignments. Since the elevation varied a lot, we were often talking about it. Sometimes 5000 feet, sometimes 15,000. Believe me, you know when you are that high up! It sucks the air out of you. One day we ended up at the Atlantic Ocean, where we would spend the night. I love blond jokes, even as a blond. But this California blond amazed everyone with her question, "I wonder what the elevation is here?" We all laughed hard as she was seriously puzzled. Dave said, "Would you please say that again?" Then he said, "...feet, above....." Oh! I could laugh as that could have easily been me.

On another day we were travelling on the Amazon River upstream on a Peki Peki which is a river taxi that got its name from the sound that the motor makes. We ended up at a village, walked up a steep and wet slope to get to the houses. We did what we came there for and in the process I could see that this was where they were making the famous "Shipibo pots." To me they are famous anyway, as our International Museum of Cultures has a story set up about how the Bible came to the Shipibo Indians and there are several Shipibo pots on display at our Museum on campus. So I had seen them for many years.

Now, right before me was the elderly lady who had made several pots. She had them on display in her shop of thatch roof with woven walls. There were about a dozen or so. I was so excited and I knew right then that I had to take one home with me. My husband said, "No" without hesitation. But, it was something that was really special to me. And besides, I confess, I like to see challenges be accomplished!!! I picked out one that was large, about three feet high and nearly that in diameter. It was beautiful. The designs on the pots are that of turtle shells. I also picked a small one that I could hand carry.

The boatman happily carried the big pot on his shoulder down the slippery hill to the boat and guarded it while he brought us back to the jungle place where we were staying. Dave and our guys built a box for it out of two by twos and Styrofoam. You could see right through it to know that it was a delicate pot and it had a secure frame. We carried it on a small plane to get back to Lima and then checked it as "luggage" for our International flight back to Dallas. It arrived just fine and this pot has been a delight to have.

Spanish Newspaper

While we were in Peru with the college students and our three sons, our fourteen-year- old daughter, Valerie, was in Taiwan and the Philippines as a companion for a Bible translator for the summer. We thought that we'd have contact regularly with her through email. But as it turned out, we could send or receive email only about once a week when we were in the larger towns. It seemed that when we were in Lima, she was out in a village. When we were out, she was in Manila. It was quite a lonely time for us all as we didn't know it was going to be like that.

One day we were at our mission guest house in Lima. Dave happened to notice the headlines in a local Spanish newspaper about a typhoon that was going through the northern most part of the Philippines. That was the exact area that we knew that Valerie was supposed to be at that time. I had no way to reach her at all. There was no way to know if she were riding out the storm, dead or alive. That was one of the hardest weeks of my life.

The day came that I knew that she was supposed to be back in Manila staying at a Guest House. I had it figured out that 7 or 8 at night in Lima was to be 7 AM in Manila and she should be getting her breakfast before leaving for another ministry at a birthing center where I used to deliver babies. I tried using a Spanish calling card at a phone booth for one whole hour to call her. I would get stuck and they were telling me a message FAST in Spanish that flew right by. I asked people to come help me with the Spanish. It kept failing and failing. Finally, after trying for one long hour I got through to the Guest House in Manila. The woman said, "Oh, she just left." I had waited a whole week to talk with her and had missed her by just a short time. I burst out in tears right then and there as only a Mother would. My very practical husband said, "At least we know that she is all right." Of course, but still as a mother this was a time to cry it out.

Once the summer was over and we could talk through the details, we learned what had happened on that end. They were out on the Island that is the furthest South in Taiwan, just north of the most Northern Philippine Islands. And indeed they all knew that a big typhoon was coming. Those few who had tickets on the planes were able to get out. It was an 18 passenger plane and just made about three trips a day. No tickets could be bought. Only those who already had tickets could get off. We knew that they were loading up ferries to bring people to safer areas. From past experience, we also knew that they sometimes overload those boats. Someone who had two tickets for a flight gave them to "his Bible translator and her friend." THAT was a sacrifice! I must say, that was someone who had been reading The Book about loving one another!!

Romans 12:10 ASV: In love of the brethren be tenderly affectioned one to another; in honor preferring one another

Randall's Motorcycle Ride

O ur son, Randall, was a missionary from the time he graduated from college and for the next few years was working in Bandung, Indonesia. Just before Christmas he let his director know that at the end of the school year he was going to be leaving. That was the system they had so they could recruit for the new staff needed for the following fall. He then came home to the US for Christmas. While he was here, there was a major Tsunami in that part of Asia, including Indonesia and Thailand. The Christmas before Randall and his room mate had stayed right on the beach at PhiPhi Island in Thailand. That was part of the area most destroyed by the storm. His room mate was there again this year with his brother from Canada. Randall didn't know how his room mate fared until a few days later, but the place they had been at the year before was already full when they arrived and he was forced uphill to another place. Randall's roommate and his brother then became a part of the recovery efforts. Both of them were spared from going out to sea.

After returning to Indonesia, Randall took a group of high school students to do crisis relief in the area that was hardest hit from the tsunami in Sumatra, the furthermost North island of Indonesia. They found out that even the high schoolers were exceptionally helpful to the relief efforts as they spoke Bahasa Indonesian. Those relief workers who had come to help with other skills needed interpreters. Before leaving the area, God was making it clear to Randall that it wasn't the right time for him to return back to the states as his skills were very much needed in Sumatra. He was willing to obey God even though he had no idea of what he would do or with what agency. He completed his term at his mission and then headed out from the mountains of Java by motorcycle to the coast, then ferried his bike across and began his ride across the southern to northern route of the long westernmost and northernmost isle of Indonesia, Sumatra.

As his mother, I had pleaded with him ahead of time to sell his bike in Bandung and buy a new one in Aceh. But, he insisted he wanted to drive it. So there he set off, white boy alone on a 2,200 kilometer route up Sumatra.

In advance, Randall arranged with an Indonesian friend that he would call each day to update where he was and be accountable to so that his friend could send out help if he wasn't heard from. The friend would then post an update for those of us following each day to Randall's blog. That was good for us to be kept informed. Then for the second week he was out, we stopped hearing from him. The days got longer and so did our prayers. When we hadn't heard from him in more than a week, one night neither Dave nor I were able to sleep. I don't think we were worried, but we were eagerly waiting to hear something. Those early morning hours slipped by and we finally went back to bed for a few hours. By 8 AM we woke and checked our email before work and found that he had written!! When we could stand it no longer, God let us hear from Randall. As it turned out, the whole northern half of the island was wiped flat from the storm and there were no cell towers left! Of course.

We didn't think of that ahead, but that made sense. According to Randall, often the only structures standing in the towns were the Mosque's. Many times he had to try to figure out where the road would have been if it were there and head that way, sometimes following rivers or other boundaries. Often the locals had made "roads" across rushing water out of a couple of coconut trees lain across the water. He would push his motorcycle while balancing on the logs, carrying his heavy backpack.

There was one day that the road was up a hill with mud to his knees, making it sluggish to push his bike. He was totally exhausted and was feeling dehydrated in the afternoon heat. He had no water left and the end of the hill was still a long ways off. He talked to God. He knew that he couldn't just set up camp and rest, he wondered if this was it. Although he hadn't seen another person on the road that day, along from the other direction came a pickup truck. The man rolled down his window, handed Randall a bottle of water!! And then he left. Was it an angel? Only God knows.

Once he came to a town, it was nearly dusk and he had the idea he was getting close to Aceh where he was trying to end up. But he was in the middle of town trying to decide if he should attempt to head into the unknown when it would soon be dark. Just resting in town, another motorcycle rider pulled up next to him and asked him if he was headed to Aceh. He said, "Yes." He said, "Follow me," and took off. Randall hustled to follow him and did so for the next five hours, in and out of security checks where they were waved right on through. As it was, this man was an aid worker who was well known by the security and God used him to grease the skids to get Randall through and in the end this stranger dropped him off right in front of where he was to stay.

He went to see the leaders from several relief ministries in the area and it wasn't too long before it was clear to him that God was leading him to be the project manager for the area for Samaritan's Purse.

Psalm 91:15 ASV: He shall call upon me, and I will answer him; I will be with him in trouble: I will deliver him, and honor him.

Isaiah 58:11 ASV: And Jehovah will guide thee continually, and satisfy thy soul in dry places, and make strong thy bones; and thou shalt be like a watered garden, and like a spring of water, whose waters fail not.

Banyon Tree

A Bible translator had come in from the province and brought his new Filipino translation
helper with him. They were attending a workshop
at the mission station and there were other national
helpers who had attended these kinds of workshops
before. This new translation worker was very excited
to learn all he could about his new work. There were
a lot of "firsts" for him, riding in an airplane, even
travelling away from his village and coming into a
"western" style setting. There was good food and
great beds.

For three weeks they had meetings, large and
small. Joint meetings with the translators and sometimes just the Filipino helpers met together. Often
this is when language helpers sometimes hear the
"Good News of the Gospel" for the first time.

When this helper returned to his village after the
meetings, he had learned so much. Every day for the
next two weeks he took his notebook full of all the
papers and the notes that he took and sat under the

Banyon tree to think about what he learned. Every day he studied the manual, thinking how to use it in his language work. One day, he got up and said, "There, now I know what to do." And he went back to work!

How smart is that! I heard that of what we hear we only retain 10%. There are multitudes of notebooks that I've collected from conferences over the years that I've had good intentions of getting back to, to glean more from all the extra input that we hadn't even gotten to in the lectures. It doesn't take long to get back into the daily grind of life and not get as much out of these as we can. I'd like to learn from him. Surely, there must be a way to slow down. So I cry out, "Lord, I need a Banyon tree."

Luke 10:39-42 ASV: And she had a sister called Mary, who also sat at the Lord's feet, and heard his word. But Martha was cumbered about much serving; and she came up to him, and said, Lord, dost thou not care that my sister did leave me to serve alone? bid her therefore that she help me. But the Lord answered and said unto her, Martha, Martha, thou art anxious and troubled about many things: but one thing is needful: for Mary hath chosen the good part, which shall not be taken away from her.

Valentine Ring

We attended a lovely Valentine's Banquet at our church put on by the youth and we had a lovely time visiting with many young couples. We are so thankful to God for the love that He's given us one to another in our marriage.

In bed that night, my finger brushed over my wedding ring only to expose an empty set of prongs where my diamond had been. I flicked on the light to confirm the truth of what I was experiencing. So I had my little "talk with Jesus." I decided that He knew where it was and if I were meant to find it, He would show me where. In the meantime, I slept soundly. Over the next few days I reminded the Lord that I loved Him and had no doubt that He loved me, so this didn't change that. And since I loved my husband and he loved me, a diamond, not even a ring was needed to prove that to anyone on this earth. I'm just a bit sentimental, and that was the only reason I felt the loss. I reminded the Lord that He told us to hold the things of this earth loosely. So I let it go. I decided this was not something to let my world be rocked by. I did do a thorough search of the house as best as I could, giving extra care in changing the bed sheets. I wondered if I would be able to feel good about ever vacuuming the carpet. But, I did it.

Oh, yes, this was also already a replacement diamond, as I had lost my original diamond. Yes, I lost my diamond the same week that I attended my father's funeral and had my purse stolen. So I determined right there that it was not good stewardship for my hubby to buy me another if I was just going to loose them. I let it go.

A few weeks later we were supposed to be going camping, but because I was really sick, Dave insisted even though we really wanted to go that we would stay home. We are very thankful on many counts for that as he got sick that same day and we both would have had the winter flu while camping. The other thing that happened is that it snowed! In Texas in March!! We would have been taking down camp the morning after it snowed, isn't it wonderful that God spared us that!!

Being home sick, I was working on a jigsaw puzzle on the card table in our family room. On my TV stand I had some hummus, so I went to get some Trisket crackers from the pantry. I took out a few and set them by the hummus and realized that there were only a few crackers left so I pulled the bag out and set it also next to the hummus. And I threw the box in the trash. I ate a few crackers. Then when I went back to my puzzle, there was a little sparkle on top of the puzzle box. It couldn't be, could it? Sure enough, my diamond dropped out of the Trisket box and right there where I could see it!!! It sat in hiding in a Trisket box for three weeks! It could have gone into the trash with the box, or what in the world was I taking the bag out of the box for anyway? Or we could have been camping. In any case, it's like finding a needle a haystack and God had shown me His great mercy once again.

Matthew 6:33 ASV: But seek ye first his kingdom, and his righteousness; and all these things shall be added unto you.

The Birth of a Ministry

In Manila twenty years ago the needs were great everywhere we went. I never could turn a blind eye, for you hurt with each one you see and wish you could help them all. When we first arrived in the Philippines I cried out to God, "How can I help so many?" He answered me that I need to be responsible for those He clearly puts in my path. I was to let Him love them through me. That was so freeing. I could say a confident yes to some and was getting practiced in saying "no."

After a few years, a friend called one day and asked if I could help her deliver babies. She had a midwifery clinic in her home to help the poor have safe and healthy deliveries. I told her that I was sorry, I had neither the time nor skills for such a thing, I wasn't a nurse. She pleaded that she just needed someone to assist and won't I please come just for the day? I agreed. And it was a really neat experience being at the other end of the delivery table after having five children of my own. It was very interesting but I wasn't in need of any extra work, I was already struggling to keep up and there's always much more I'd like to do if I had the time. Ministry opportunities abound in Manila.

Within a few days she called again. I did see the need for the ministry she was doing and empathized with her need. Even though these were busy days, at the time she called I didn't have anything just then crying out for my time. So I agreed again and a couple more times after that, always with the idea that I was helping out in a pinch and had no intention of getting hooked into this.

That the ministry was needed was no question. When these women are living in their home provinces (the country) they have the advantage of the help of their female relatives to support them and help with the delivery of their babies. They come to Manila with what I call the "Hollywood syndrome." Hope for a good job that will supply the needs of the entire family in the province overshadows the reality of the impossibility of getting a job. There are ten million people who live in Manila and eighty five percent made less than the poverty wage that was equivalent to one dollar per day.* Poverty was rampant. Instead of having a dream job, many end up stuck in Manila without even enough money to return home. I must say that much of this has improved in many ways since then.

They lived in rough made shanties, from whatever materials they could scrounge. Then when they are to have their babies, they have no money to go to the hospital and no longer have sisters, mothers and aunts to help them. The mortality rate in childbirth is very high. So when my friend discovered a squatter village near her home had a need, she started out to help one lady, who then brought a friend and so on until she now has a three bed clinic in her home and does prenatal and postnatal care. Many of the supplies we used are provided by other ministries.

I had been praying that our fourteen year old daughter, Nicole, and I could have something that we could do together. I was thinking of a craft or something. With our busy paces we often had little quality time to spend together. I was thinking that in a few years we'd be sending her back to the States for college. After I'd gone a few times to deliver babies, Nicole expressed an interest in helping too. And it has turned into a wonderful ministry for us to do together. I learned that my daughter was very gentle and compassionate and capable of quickly following instructions responsibly. This ministry has been quite a gift from God.

One day still early on, we were helping with the birth of a little boy. His mother was fifteen years old. She had her arms around my neck and was laboring long and hard. She finally squatted and her baby was born. We were waiting to cut the cord until after the placenta was delivered. It was really nice to have that transition time. We taught the mothers to take and hold their babies right away and bond with them. We were waiting on the placenta. Something hadn't coagulated properly and burst and was like an explosion of blood, covering lots in the room. My friend shouted to quick get the baby out of here. I quickly cut the cord and Nicole and I rushed him out to clean him up. We pleaded for the life of the mother the whole while the nurse worked to massage the uterus.

After we cleaned the baby, Nicole and I cleaned ourselves up a bit and returned with a cold wet towel, (we didn't have hot tap water there) to try to get some of the blood off the midwife and the mother. As I was washing the mother, a strong picture of Jesus, *washing the feet of His disciples* came over me. It was so clear, Jesus was telling me that this WAS a work He was calling me to do. I had neither the skills nor the time (I thought). If we believe Jesus' words that, "I can do all things through Christ who strengthens me," then it is our very weaknesses that He will use to bring glory to Himself, through us.

The mother did live and I know she'd have surely died had she been at home. Every life is valuable to Jesus.

*This was from the late 1980's. I'm happy to report that the poverty is not as great at this time in Manila as we see many more middle class families.

2 Corinthians 12:9 ASV: And he hath said unto me, My grace is sufficient for thee: for my power is made perfect in weakness. Most gladly therefore will I rather glory in my weaknesses, that the power of Christ may rest upon me.

Sailing

We did what missionaries call "hitting the ground running." Following an intense time of wrapping things up in the Philippines to prepare to return to our home country, we needed to keep running to get as much done over the summer months as we could before settling in for the school year.

Before leaving the foreign field you run on adrenaline and anticipation of "coming home." There are a million details to attend to about storing our belongings, getting some to send home if not returning, some to dispose if something happens. Also the need to arrange a speaking schedule with home churches and figuring out some kind of gifts that we can afford to bring many people without breaking the bank.

We got a car in California and Dave and the boys were driving it back to Texas while we girls flew. We gathered our boxes that we had in storage and choose what things would travel with us for the summer months in Minnesota. Mostly that meant fishing gear and the rifles the boys had been waiting to see. We had a couple of days turn around time in Dallas once the guys arrived and then headed directly to a cabin in Minnesota.

Just a couple of days to settle in before we started our summer visiting with our supporters and churches all over Minnesota. Each time we would return to the cabin we would crash and try to rest and recover before leaving again. We were still experiencing the stresses of changing cultures again.

Once at the cabin, we could do jigsaw puzzles or read or just look out at the lake or splash in the water. The children were eager to fish and do all kinds of other things that needed our help until they learned how to do them so we were kept busy.

There was also a sailboat at the cabin. I have always loved to sail. I just didn't have the energy to even go out. Randall was the first to figure out how to rig the sails and take it out. It took his help and five weeks of rest before I was ready to venture out.

Once I did it was wonderfully freeing! Back and forth, dipping and tacking. I had so much fun and found it relaxing. In bed that night, the feeling of floating across the water was still with me. The feeling of sailing in my bed brought the thought that my life was a lot like that sail. My sail is up, and the Holy Spirit was filling it to blow wherever He was leading me with firm and gentle power. That is how the summer felt. "Yes, Lord, blow as You will!"

John 3:8 ASV: The wind bloweth where it will, and thou hearest the voice thereof, but knowest not whence it cometh, and whither it goeth: so is every one that is born of the Spirit.

Reservations, Really?

For Christmas break we gathered a group of five families to travel together from Manila to our favorite beach resort. We had been there two months ahead of time and asked over and again, now you will hold the entire resort for us between Christmas and New Years, correct?

It's a full travel day. First a two and a half hour bus trip from Manila to Batangas. Next a two hour ferry boat to the island pier. From the pier we took 4 Bangkas (outrigger boats) to the resort. Coming into view of the resort we could see people around and towels hanging from the balcony's of our huts. On shore we met to talk with the owners. What ever we thought we had agreed on didn't obviously pan out. So all of us waited on shore trying to think up what we would now do. It was too late to return to Manila and it was evident that we'd need to make new plans.

This was busy season so all the other resorts would also be full. One of the boatmen had the best idea. His family island was not too far away. How would we all like to come there for our vacation? How thankful we were for an option like that!

We boarded the bangkas again and moved to the near-by island. Upon landing the children got busy doing what kids do in the sand, burying people, making castles. We adults were escorted around the island to see what options we had for places to stay. One family offered to let a family stay in their home with them. There were a few vacant homes with bare cement block to sleep on that worked for a few more. Somehow we all made it work and it was a lovely adventure we'll never forget.

The real excitement came, though, in watching the island folks figure out how to feed the multitudes. The people were so kind, they treated us like royalty. They put together a nice meal for us. Silverware and plates were collected from all over town and a large table was some boards set on horses in the middle of town with dirt as our floor. The little children hid behind trees or huts to watch the foreigners eat and talk. We must have been quite a sight for them. They repeated this the next day for both breakfast and lunch. The boatmen came by to inform us that the resort had made arrangements for the other guests and wanted us to return for the rest of our vacation. We did, but nothing would ever compare to these kind people who all pitched together to welcome us and bless us with their hospitality and love.

Hebrews 13:2 ASV: Forget not to show love unto strangers: for thereby some have entertained angels unawares.

On Being An
Accountant Missionary

D ave was the manager of the Accounting department for the International Linguistics center
in Dallas, a post that he held for about twelve years.
Being a volunteer mission organization, all of the
staff are on what is called "Faith Support" and are all
missionaries. That included the accounting people.
There came a time when BOTH of the other accountants working under Dave's leadership decided to
leave the mission organization. They had been missionaries about the same amount of time that we
had. It's always so hard when someone has to leave
especially when the reason is finances. That hurts all
the more when there is SO much wealth in the USA.
Missionary accountants often are short on funds.
We have always been very thankful to God for our
teams' recognition of the importance of having professional accountants manage for the Lords work
as in any credible organization. For them to see the

98

need for how we fit in to the work of Bible translation is vital.

Being short staffed has an emotional effect on us
as we grieved the loss of two good families to the
mission. Both of these men had invaluable experience and left over money. So Dave picked up their
work load and added a couple of students to fill in
some of the gaps. The bulk of the loss still rested on
Dave.

When we first learned of these two leaving we
wondered if we would have the faith and the stamina
to continue on in ministry ourselves. We kept
acknowledging that we trusted God and we counted
on Him to see us through all of the changes. Things
got progressively worse for us. We had a hard time
paying our bills and we suffered greatly trying to
stretch our funds, sometimes close to giving up.
Each time we sought God concerning our leaving
the mission, He gave us a picture of Esau giving up
his birthright for something that would perish. We
never felt as if God freed us to leave.

God used a vision in my quiet time during this
period that helped to begin to fan the flames of hope
for both of us. In that moment He assured me that I
would one day again have a ministry to the poor. If
I wanted to be able to minister His love to others,
I needed to identify with those by knowing how it
feels to suffer much. There was something so precious and comforting to me to know that there was
a reason for the suffering. That made it easier to
"embrace" the pain and willingly bear it instead of

trying to avoid it. In so doing, God was showing me that He was preparing me to live again in a third world ministry. I was unhappy about being called to be a missionary in Dallas, and I had not surrendered to God to minister HERE. In fact, I was rather upset with God that He had called us into a mission career and then stuck us in the states, in the buckle of the Bible belt.

I felt like I was drowning. I knew that I could not rescue myself from the problems going on in my life. I knew that only if God picked me up again was there any hope of new life. When I finally surrendered to obey His will instead of my own, He pumped NEW JOY into my life again.

Since this decision, so much has changed. God is blessing us in so many areas. Ministry opportunities are the majors again instead of the minors in our lives. He is again providing miraculously for our needs. He has given us a few new supporters, always a need in missions, and He has replaced our 'Beverly Hillbilly' style car with a newer van.

Caring friends have blessed us in numerous ways. We are encouraged through our team more than any of them know. A fresh flow of God's amazing love in our hearts has lifted us up to continue going forward "by faith."

Philippians 4:19 ASV: And my God shall supply every need of yours according to his riches in glory in Christ Jesus.

Thanksgiving in Mexico

Thanksgiving was special for us that year. Our family was in the process of a three month training program for new missionaries to prepare us for the foreign mission field. We had a combination of camp time with learning experiences in cross-cultural living. For six weeks we stayed in a small cabin with the John out back before moving into Mexico to live with a family there for four more weeks. At one time we had seventeen people living under one roof in a Mexican home with one bathroom! We practiced our Spanish and homeschooled our kids while continuing to learn about living cross culturally. The next phase was to learn to get around on public transportation. We were to cover a certain number of kilometers over ten days using various types of public transportation and could only stay in one place for two nights. We took an all night bus from the border town into Mexico City and visited with a pastor that was a relative of our host family. We attended his home church and shared Sunday dinner together. While we were in the service, our kids were romping around the second floor balcony with the other kids. There were NO guard rails and my kids were young and not used to such a thing, but we had to stay in our place of honor at the service and trust them into God's care. From where I sat I could see my three preschoolers and one elementary age daughter going in and out of windows, and running on the balcony. God had His angels on special duty that day.

In the morning before we left our hotel room, we laid out the map to decide where we were to go next. We had picked out three possibilities that were in equal range away and we knew nothing about any of them, so we prayed that God would lead us. After lunch, the pastor asked us where we were heading next. We said that we are praying about it. He suggested, practically insisted, that we head to Cuernavaca. That was one of the three cities we had chosen so we followed his guidance.

Arriving in Cuernavaca, we took two taxis to a hotel along with luggage for seven. The hotel did not have two adjoining rooms so they would not allow us to stay with our large family. They recommended another place across town that might work for us. Dave hailed another taxi and at least this one was a van so we all fit in one. Where he took us was actually a retreat center with simple and very comfortable rooms, a dining hall and nice courtyard where we could all wander. It was lovely with poinsettias and bougainvilleas and was a welcome and refreshing rest stop for our souls. We were enjoying visiting with the other guests.

After dinner one of the hosts invited us to join them for dinner the next night. They told us that the missionaries from around the area were gathering for a Thanksgiving Potluck meal and fun night together. We hadn't even realized that it was Thanksgiving as we'd been so busy on the road. Here again, we were led by God to be where He wanted us to be, with the added blessing of celebrating our holiday with our brothers and sisters in Christ. A blessing that we didn't even know we needed, was known ahead by God. All of us are carried in the palm of His hands and He knows every need we have. Each Thanksgiving I remember that Thanksgiving and the special way God had for us.

Psalm 100:4-5 ASV: Enter into his gates with thanksgiving, And into his courts with praise: Give thanks unto him, and bless his name. For Jehovah is good; his lovingkindness endureth for ever, And his faithfulness unto all generations.

Paul And Randall's Sailing Adventure

We were at the cabin of some friends of ours in Minnesota where we spent many happy summer hours. A variety of outdoor recreation and sports were the delight of us all.

The boys beat me to the sailboat. For someone who loves to sail, that was good!! It took me five weeks back in the US to relax and rest enough to have the strength to start venturing out that much.

Randall has lots of courage. He figured out how to rig the sails without instruction and headed out. He was delightfully surprised when he was able to go out and return back, developing a regular course. Even when he capsized he was able to right the boat.

A few days after this he and Paul had gone out at a time when the wind was really strong. They travelled clear across the lake before the sail tipped over into the water. They attempted to right it, but the wind was so strong it whipped it right back under. Now they started to get afraid. They kept trying but could not get the sail upright. Finally, Randall said to his brother, "Let's pray." They closed their eyes and when they opened them on "Amen," they said they looked on shore and there was a woman looking at them with her binoculars. She called to them that she didn't have a boat but would call someone who did to come and help them. They were startled at how fast God had answered their prayer. Finally, a couple with a pontoon boat came to the rescue. It took a long time to get the sail out of the mud in the bottom of the lake but they eventually did and tied the boat to the side of the pontoon. The nice couple delivered them to our shore. They said that they'd rescued a couple of canoes before, but this was the first time they'd come to rescue a sailboat.

Thanks, Lord, for teaching our children that when they pray, You answer.

1 John 5:14-15 ASV: And this is the boldness which we have toward him, that, if we ask anything according to his will, he heareth us: and if we know that he heareth us whatsoever we ask, we know that we have the petitions which we have asked of him.

Holy Boldness

During our first training with Wycliffe, we attended a camp in the mountains in Idyllwild California for five weeks with about forty other missionary candidates. There was cross cultural training, language learning, and focusing our prayer to the will of God. Before we arrived we had already filled out mountains of paper work. We'd send them a pile and they'd send a whole other batch. They had references of everyone we know. This time on the mountain was a time for The Mission Leadership to observe our family and see if they found us "fit" for missionary service. We waited for them to send us home. We were also prayerfully seeking God about whether he had indeed called us into service as missionaries. This was pretty serious stuff and we put the whole future of our family into God's hands and waited to see how He would lead.

We were kept very busy. We had four children at this time and one of the things I remember is getting them in and out of snowsuits over and over every day. We lived in a small cabin at the bottom of a hill. The dining hall was up the hill. There was snow so we needed the cold weather outerwear. It was hot in the dining hall, so we took off four snowsuits before sitting down to breakfast. Then we dressed them all again to return down the hill for their schools and nursery. We trekked back up the hill to our class. Lunch was the same thing, downhill, snowsuits, uphill, snowsuits off, snowsuits on, down, snowsuits off. You get the picture.

Our little home was one room with a bed in it and a table with four chairs. There was a large closet sized room that had a bunk bed, with a day bed between it and the wall and a crib at the top of the bunk and the wall. It was wall to wall beds. In order for the kids to sleep, we had to leave the door open a crack so it wasn't pitch black. But we couldn't have too much light on in the main room either. Dave and I did our studying over the toilet in the only room that had light after bedtime. Every night.

With all that was involved in the mission training and the care of the children, we were nose to the grindstone, no personal time and we fell in bed each night at one or two.

Imagine how surprised we were to find out that we were expecting baby number five after our time on the hill! We were already asking God, "Are You really calling us to the mission field with four children?" Surprise: not four but five! It was an impossible situation to be in. Now we would be trusting God 100% for everything we would need to do His work. If He can provide for four, He knows what He's doing and can provide for five children!

We were accepted and eagerly began the next step of the process which was to go share this good news with everybody we knew and raise our support. God was asking us to be a part in taking His Word to those from every nation, tongue and tribe so that all could understand His love letter in their heart language. The Word of God is for everyone! It is the base for all other mission work.

When it was time to deliver our precious new bundle, we were still in Minnesota raising our support.

In the delivery process they gave me a glucose IV. Once Valerie was born it was becoming cumbersome to hold her while still attached with a board to an IV in my arm. I asked the nurse if she would come and please remove it. She gave me all the reasons why I needed to keep it attached. I called her back a few minutes later and told her that I was now going to hold my baby without the board, so either she could come and remove it or I would take care of doing so.

I thought about that later. To do the kind of pioneer work that we do takes a certain level of boldness. One needs to be strong through many difficult things, so I figure that God was already stretching me to be bold outside of my comfort zone through this. And He has!

2 Timothy 1:7 ASV: For God gave us not a spirit of fearfulness; but of power and love and discipline.

We're Home

After our Quest experience in California having been living in a fishbowl and learning more about Wycliffe, we all came to the same conclusion that God was leading us to a future with this mission, Wycliffe Bible Translators. After the training was over and we were accepted as members of Wycliffe, we prayed before leaving the Mountains that God would make His will clear to us as to where we would serve and doing what. We felt wide open and vulnerable to the plans that our leaders felt where we were needed most to further Bible Translation.

There was a recruiter who made a trip up from the Huntington Beach office to the training facility to talk with us about where Dave could be used in the accounting end of the ministry. He asked us to come out to California for another part of our pre-field training.

While we were at Quest, we randomly signed up to share our story with the group of how it was that we were now here at this place in our lives. How had

God led us and we heard incredible tales night after night. On the night that we shared there was a man who had driven the 110 miles up to show someone who was visiting the headquarters in LA our training facility. They arrived in time for the meeting and after we shared, he jumped up and introduced himself and said that he prays to the Lord of the harvest to send out laborers and reminds God that, "we need accountants, too." And here you are!! He prayed with us right then. We were eager to visit with him after the meeting was over but by then he had left to get back home. We didn't know his name or who he was.

Once our training was over, we prayed that God would make it clear what our next step should be. Then we spent a few days in Huntington Beach California where our US Wycliffe offices were before heading back to Minnesota. It was a stress filled few days and we figured that the change from our little "cocoon" environment and now being back to a normal environment was just an adjustment we'd need to make.

A bit out of our way heading back to Minnesota, we decided to swing through Dallas to see our International Headquarters. When we drove through the entrance of the center, we both had this strong feeling come over us, hard to explain, but we both felt like "we're home." Odd, we had no connection here, except that the pre-field coordinator that we'd been assigned to work with worked out of Dallas. We went to see him and told him about the strange experience coming into the center. "Oh, then you need to talk with the Vice President of Finance," said he. He walked us across the compound and introduced us to the VPF. It was the man who had been at the meeting we shared at in the mountains in California! He confirmed to us that God had surely led us to do our pre-field work in Dallas instead of California. This was a time to learn more about how the mission operates to prepare for overseas.

Psalm 32:8 ASV: I will instruct thee and teach thee in the way which thou shalt go: I will counsel thee with mine eye upon thee.

New Is Sometimes Hard

When we were away from the USA for four years, a lot of things had changed. I guess that we had also!!

My sister and her son picked us up from the airport. I rode with her while the rest of the family went with her son and our families' twenty one bags rode in another friends van.

My first clue that things would be different for me was while we were still at the airport. I got in my sisters little sports car and she told me to buckle the seatbelt. We didn't even have seatbelts in our van in the Philippines. So I searched for it and attempted to put it on, unsuccessfully. She reached across and pulled it and handed it to me, but before I could find where to plug it in, it had tightened too much and I ended up letting it go. Now it was starting to make us laugh. She tried that again I think, and since I still didn't get it in before it snapped in too tight, she decided to come around the car and pull it, and hand it to me. She did, but before she got back to her seat,

I had let it go so she had to come around again. That is such a little thing, but we were laughing hysterically before we left that lot.

While we were gone the look of the cars had changed. Before we left they were boxy still and they were rounded by the time we returned.

Visiting with a friend up at her lake home, I made a call to talk with my dad. Imagine my surprise when the phone was able to come with me all the way from the kitchen to the hammock where I hung out and visited with my Dad. That was no big deal to them, but it sure was different for us. Sometimes we had to drive across Manila traffic because it was more dependable than calling.

We stayed in a cabin that had been supplied with paper goods and food. The plastic cups were very nice and I was washing them until my friend came in and asked what I was doing that for? They were to make it easy for me, so they were to be used and then thrown away. Oh, my. How can I learn to throw away? Change can be hard.

Another friend that we visited had a machine that she could just put in all the bread ingredients and set the time that she wanted it ready and push a button and we would have fresh bread when dinner was ready.

I was asked paper or plastic at the market. What in the world did that mean?

The classic that my friends got a kick out of was within the first week we were back I needed to get shampoo. Where I came from there were just a few simple choices. But at the drug store, there was a whole isle dedicated to the many choices of shampoo. Oh, I got excited about that. Looking at one after the other, I started to get overwhelmed by the choices. Finally, I saw one that said, "for permed hair." That was amazing, I decided that this was the one. The rest of my family could use that kind that was special for me. When I got home and looked at the bottle, my gut hurt, for it was conditioner and not even Shampoo. Ouch.

Then there was the butter. We could choose butter or margarine, one kind each. Here we had so many choices it boggled my mind. Liquid, spray, tubs of all sorts. There was much more for me to learn.

We bought a washer and dryer and put them into our home. I went to load the washer and looked for how to put in the water, and found that I had loaded the dryer. It really is that different.

Before we came home someone said that they felt like a stranger in their own country. I felt that way for a time.

Now, lest you think I'm the only one who would do these weird things, here's the next generations turn! Nicole was offered the option to ride to school with a neighbor rather than taking the bus, an option she jumped on. When they arrived at school she tried to unlock the belt but couldn't find the latch. She sat there a while and finally it occurred to him why she wasn't getting out. He chuckled and showed her. The belt was released by opening the door! Well, we eventually do learn!! We can't take ourselves too seriously. We must have a sense of humor.

Proverbs 17:22 ASV: A cheerful heart is a good medicine; But a broken spirit drieth up the bones.

Speeding Through Life

For many years, the pace in which we lived was fast and furious. Moving back and forth across the world with a family of seven and settling in each time was a challenge. That is in addition to the work itself. There was never a dull moment. One summer we took our children to see parts of our Nations History in the DC area while on a trip to see supporters in the Northeast. We were gone a couple of weeks and that included some time in Chicago and a few more days in Minnesota before heading back to Texas. We were pushing, moving and shaking fast the whole time.

The stretch from Washington DC to West of Chicago was the longest push day, seventeen hours, only stopping for bathroom, gas and food breaks. I was focused when it was my time to drive. I set the cruise and headed west. So focused, I just kept my eye on the goal, Chicago. At some point I became aware that there was a policeman behind me with his lights on so I figured I better move over a lane and let him pass by.

He moved over behind me still with his lights flashing. So I decided I'd pull to the side to see if he wanted me and if not, he'd just move on. He stopped. I was totally clueless. I got into the squad car, gave him my license, and he proceeded to ask me questions. Where I was going and do I know what speed was I travelling, etc. He had been following me with his lights on for two miles before I noticed him. I had come into a city area where the speed decreases by ten miles and I was flying past others and not even noticing. I told him about our long trek. My record came up clean so he asked me, "If I let you go, do you think that you can get out of Ohio without getting yourself noticed again?" What I said was, "Yes, sir." What I thinking was, "Oh, am I in Ohio?"

Shepherd or Hireling

D ue to being sick, I was sleeping soundly when the phone rang. It was my son, Randall, calling to ask if I was watching the news. He and his new bride lived near downtown Dallas on the Trinity River. They were in a ministry called "Apartment Life." Randall worked from an office in his apartment and was startled by the blasts from across the river where a chemical supply business had caught fire. His home started shaking with great intensity. He said that it sounded like a war zone. He went out to watch and then started calling people.

Now awake, I sat glued to the TV to watch the ordeal. There was much that amazed me. Having the plant away from downtown was a wise engineering move. As the flames torched the sky, it was astounding that it was not burning the bridges around it. It was contained in the area set aside for this chemical plant.

The police immediately shut down the freeway, a big artery into Dallas. We later heard that 900,000 people were affected by the traffic delay. Canisters of gas became projectiles onto the freeways, and there were secondary explosions. Grass fires were started here and there, and one could see many fire-fighting troops waiting in the wings, unable to enter this volatile situation.

The film crew showed the beginning phases of this event that had turned into what looked like an atomic attack. It all started with a faulty coupler near a tank truck. The driver recognized the danger and ran outside immediately.

Just after the fire started, there was a water hose visible on the left side of the truck pointing into the semi tank, making a valiant effort to control the fire. But another nearby tank blew and when the smoke cleared you could again see the hose, trying to keep the fire in check. It was amazing to see that the water spray from the hose looked smaller and smaller as the flames grew. My heart immediately went out to the person behind that hose.

Soon there were many tanks flaming and gaseous flames shot sky-high. Surely now the person behind the hose would recognize the futility of his efforts and run for his life. The smoke would clear and there again would be this tiny trickle of fire hose aimed at the massive flames.

Unbelievably, no one was killed except the 3 guard dogs from the property, some of man's best friends. Three men were taken to a hospital with severe burns as apparently this gas, Acentimine, is the hottest burning gas and is used for welding and mixing into other gasses when extra heat was needed. One of the three people burned was one of the owners of the company. We later learned that he was the brave man behind the water hose.

I recognized a Biblical principle behind this event. The owner, like the Good Shepherd who laid down his life for his sheep, went the second mile and tried as hard as possible to contain this disaster. The truck driver knew his life was at risk and did what was natural to protect his own safety.

What an incredible responsibility we who are shepherds of God's flock have, to make sure that we do all we can to see that none under our care fall away. This owner did not abandon his cause, even at great peril to his own life.

John 10:11-15 ASV: I am the good shepherd: the good shepherd layeth down his life for the sheep. He that is a hireling, and not a shepherd, whose own the sheep are not, beholdeth the wolf coming, and leaveth the sheep, and fleeth, and the wolf snatcheth them, and scattereth [them]:[he fleeth] because he is a hireling, and careth not for the sheep. I am the good shepherd; and I know mine own, and mine own know me, even as the Father knoweth me, and I know the Father; and I lay down my life for the sheep.

Four Prayer Requests

We had just done some travelling around the United States to visit with friends and supporters, and what a privilege that is. Day after day, we were able to see and have great conversations with those we love and who love our Lord. It's very special – we feel so rich! No matter how hard we try, in every area we go to we still always miss people that we'd like to see. I can't wait until heaven when time will never be an issue anymore.

In our Christmas letter that year, we had four specific financial needs that we shared with our support team. While on the road, we were marveling about the wonderful way that God had answered three out of four of these needs. We decided that the fourth was really more of a "want" than a need, so we were content. That fourth was for God to make a way for us to travel to Indonesia to see our son who was a missionary there. We missed him and wanted to have the blessing of seeing him in his "God ordained" environment.

Once back home, we called up all of the email that had accumulated while we were on the road for the five previous days. In that mail was a note from Randall. The principal at his school asked Randall if his dad would come and help all of the missionaries there with their taxes. Randall had his dad do his taxes each year and there was something he did that the others didn't know about and it was a big issue that they needed to get resolved. WOW, God fulfilled that fourth miracle request also! Praise Him! We believe that God doesn't do things partway, so if He provided for Dave to go, surely He would make a way for me to go also. All four of those special needs were met in a very short time. And how we loved our time in Indonesia with our son!

Matthew 7:7-8 ASV: Ask, and it shall be given you; seek, and ye shall find; knock, and it shall be opened unto you: for every one that asketh receiveth; and he that seeketh findeth; and to him that knocketh it shall be opened.

Lost in the Woods

W here we lived in Dallas, there was a large wooded area behind our house that the children used for all kinds of adventure and fun, as well as for learning good life lessons.

Nearly every day after school and all weekend, our kids along with half of the neighborhood found their way venturing further and further into the depths of the woods, clearing the brush to make trails throughout. They had a highway system developed that included brush and rocky terrain and avoided swamps. Building forts of various types was also part of the experience.

The forts had caused a few family squabbles. Most were "secret." One would tell the other, "You weren't supposed to tell anybody" and the other would reply, "You weren't supposed to tell anyone where mine is either."

Dave and I like to take our walks in the woods also. One day we told our kids we were headed out and our daughter started to cry. She had worn her new shoes into the woods that day and took them off and then was not able to find them. And to make matters worse, she and her friend had gotten terribly lost in the woods trying to find them and they had cried together in the woods over that.

We told her that we were glad that she told us about her problem so we could try to help her solve it. She was almost afraid to tell us because they were new shoes. What if we were mad at her for losing them? We reminded her that we would love her no matter what happened to her shoes. We prayed, "Lord, please give us eyes to see them and help Valerie to remember where they are."

She had already gone back in to look for them with her brother and so was convinced she didn't know where to look. "So, which way did you go into the woods?" She knew where she entered so we started there. "We turned to the right." "That's good." Stop. "Remember, we were lost mommy?" "Did you sit down to take them off?" "Yes, there were two stumps and there was a little prickle bush between the stumps. When I sat down I had to get back up because of the prickles." Were they big stumps or little, lying down on the ground or standing up?"

Our little girl shared that they had to take their shoes off. The Indians always went through the woods quietly and the shoes were noisy.

"Here's where we were crying, Mommy, when we were lost and I prayed. And then we found out that we were near to an entrance so we went out."

Dave saw up ahead, between two stumps, one pair of shoes, a coloring book and a ziplock bag of crayons. What a happy little girl. Just like Jesus helped her find her way out of the woods, He also cared about her feelings about the lost shoes and helped her find them, too. We thanked God together for His special care.

After bringing Valerie back home, we then headed back into the woods. Randall met us this time and wanted to know if we'd like to see his new fort. They had cleared the paths with hatchets and machetes and we went back a half-mile at least. The fort they had built this time was a full 10X10 feet, mostly woven saplings to create the walls and roof. They filled them in with cedar boughs – quite impressive. Over the entrance they had a booby trap for the unsuspecting invader. There was also a grate hanging from the wall that they had used recently to cook burgers over an open fire. Also there was a lookout tower high up to spy on the enemy. This is what they meant when they said, "I'm going out to my fort!"

We also learned from the boys that they too sometimes found themselves lost. Paul said that he could always tell his direction from the sun. Randall listened for the traffic noise and headed the other direction. Again, we thanked God for these woods where they could create and have those kinds of adventures.

Luke 15:24 ASV: ...for this my son was dead, and is alive again; he was lost, and is found. And they began to be merry.

An Artist

For years I've talked with other parents about the giftedness of artistic children. With two of our five children being especially artistic, it occurred to me that it was more difficult for them to decide on a career path. They are interested in so many things and are so creative that they can excel in several areas, making it hard to want to narrow the field down to just one routine that they will use to "make a living." Now that both of them are really enjoying the blessing of using their skills, a new thought has come to me.

Contrast this with our son, Paul, who left high school a year early as he was eager to pursue his Accounting career. He knew what he wanted and went for it with gusto, and by knowing as a freshman that he was going to pursue his masters and CPA, he was able to get into an accelerated program that gave him both his undergraduate degree and MBA by the time he was 22 years old. He had also gained five years of experience in a CPA firm before moving from college into his career. Randall also knew what he wanted, headed to college with full gusto, and finished his degree easily in four years before heading to the mission field, where he would gain lots of leadership experience before coming back to work in the United States. Valerie was on task since she was four years old to become a doctor. All through school she knew where she was headed and got college scholarships to pursue her career choice. Actually, along the way, she changed direction to that of paramedic, recognizing that her passion was really in the first line contact for emergencies. So she got her BA in Biology/Pre-med and went on to become a Licensed Paramedic.

For my oldest, an artist, it took until she was 32 years old before she was working in an art profession that would really pay her bills. To watch her struggle over the years, while she discovered that, was not easy as parents, but we encouraged her that using her gifts would bring her more fulfillment than making money somewhere she was miserable. Ecclesiastics 3:22 says, *"Wherefore I saw that there is nothing better, than that a man should rejoice in his works; for that is his portion."*

Ben is our other artist. He is trained in graphic design and is a guitarist. He would love to earn a living by playing music, and I know he is not alone in that. But, he is also skilled in computer work and after getting his foot in the door at a national company, he was quickly promoted to the Director's area of the company to be right-hand-man in the office administration.

At the ripe old age of 54, I started to realize something about myself. For years my job had everything to do with making a home and meeting the needs of our family of seven as we moved and changed between the banking world and missions, both at home and abroad. My work was very fast-paced and I never had to wonder what to do to "fill time." I never had time to be bored. There were far too many wonderful things I would have loved to do if I had the time.

Now all five children are grown and the youngest graduated from college. My life commitments have changed and God has led me into a job that I just love. It is one with incredible variety, which is how I like it. Some of my tasks have been "artistically" related, and all of a sudden, I'm realizing how much I'm enjoying that creative side of life. A few years before I got back into the working world, I did a career guidance assessment to see where I would work best. I have always wondered "what I'd do when I grow up!" I enjoyed being a homemaker and always had plenty to keep me more than satisfied. Being in missions, I knew there would be a place where I could contribute those same skills I had used to motivate my family on to excellence. One of the things that the woman who did the assessment said was that I had a lot of artistic skills. I didn't think so since I was unable to draw, paint, or anything of that sort.

One day when Nicole was in high school, she set me up with an easel and palate of paint and told me to "just paint what you see, you know, the lines, the shadows, etc." I dabbed with no creativity, so I decided I wasn't an artist.

My boss put me in charge of creating a "Learning Center" from the materials that were given to us from another location. I had some pictures of what it was like at its old home, but had to figure out how to make it usable in our new space. This was a time of incredible passion and creativity. Day and night I thought about where each piece would go, kind of like a museum curator. By the time I had nailed my last item, I felt great about it and was receiving comments back from other people about how much they loved the change from the basic four square walls to the museum look that tells our story. Well, I couldn't take the credit as others created the displays. And our Director had the foresight to go to them when they were closing and ask if we might have the displays for our mission's international office here in Dallas. I simply had the pleasure of putting these great materials together.

Now that it was set up, the thought came to me, "Like my artistic children, it has taken me even longer to discover what my area of gifted passion is. Maybe I too am an artist."

Prior to her current job, Nicole was working as a chef for a health food restaurant, creating meals that were healthy and unique. She found that expressing herself through the art of cooking was rewarding for that season. I asked her about that, as she really wasn't interested in cooking while she was at home, but she said, "I watched you Mom!" HMM, is cooking also an art?

Another experience that I had was to put together flower arrangements for Valentine's Day. With no experience in that area, my friend and I managed to create 80 lovely baskets and vases of various forms, all in one day! I guess there is some latent artistic ability in me, after all. Some artists take a very long time to find that – I did!

"Great works are performed not by strength but by perseverance." – Samuel Johnson

"Then he said to me, "This is what the LORD says to Zerubbabel: It is not by force nor by strength, but by my Spirit, says the LORD of Heaven's armies." Zachariah 4:6

How They Met

The young woman who had been our house-helper in Manila let us know six months ahead of time that she was getting married. She wanted us to come to the Philippines and to sponsor her wedding. We told her it was an honor and that we'd love to do this, but it was very expensive to fly to Manila and we could not afford the travel. We had been away from the Philippines for sixteen years and had always wanted to return.

She very much wanted us to be there, so she said she would pray that we would be able to come. We asked Randall if he could go over from Indonesia to attend on our behalf. But it happened that he had a conference planned at the same time. So no one from our family would be able to be there. Finally, after she told us a few more times that she was praying, we decided that we too ought to be praying to that end.

Whenever we are asking something special from the Lord that requires extra finances, we start an envelope and deposit "extra" funds that are not designated for our regular ministry expenses. The day after Christmas of 2006 we decided that there was enough in the envelope to start considering looking for tickets. The first time we looked, there was a 'buy one, get one free' special. We love those kinds of bargains! And we felt as if this was God's indication that we were to go to the wedding. In fact, the exact amount that we needed – to the dollar – was in the envelope. We bought the tickets and set the date for our time in the Philippines. We were hoping that we could also include a trip to see Randall in Indonesia during this time, but the added cost made that prohibitive.

The week before we arrived, Randall let us know that his plans had changed and his conference was rescheduled, so he was now able to come to the Philippines also. We were so happy at how God allowed this to work out.

We arrived on a Friday night at the Guest House of SIL in Manila. That same night, two young ladies from Dallas also arrived and we met them at breakfast. The younger of the two, Hanna, had just graduated from the same school in Arlington, Texas, from which Paul and Valerie had graduated. Hanna knew Val who was two years ahead of her. The other young lady was Ryanna. She had been the director of a Christian preschool for a few years and was travelling along with Hanna to work at five different mission places that year. It turned out that she lived only a few houses away from Rachel, our other daughter-in-law, in Texas. She and Valerie had been on a mission trip together a few years earlier, so Valerie knew her.

The two young gals, a few other SIL ladies and I went on a shopping spree that Saturday around Manila. Arriving back at the guest house at supper time, I thought that surely Randall would have arrived from Indonesia by then. It wasn't until we were almost finished eating that the cab pulled up outside the dining room and I raced out to hug my son, and told him, "Wait until you meet these young ladies, one's even from Duncanville!" Even after spending the day together, in my excitement I couldn't remember Ryanna's name to introduce her, or maybe "jetlag" was my excuse. But they met and we visited awhile.

Randall quickly ran out back to see if his name was still in the cement where he had written it as a youth. It said, Randall/Aaron July 31, 1990. He came in excited to tell about that.

The next morning we attended a Filipino church with the engaged couple, and when we broke for Sunday School, Randall attended with the young adults. Before we left, he had seven invitations from the ladies to come back that night for their Valentine Banquet. He went back, with the two new ladies.

As Randall tells the story, the others all thought that Randall and Ryanna were boyfriend/girlfriend and didn't believe they had just met. They played some games that sounded a bit risky for just meeting, like the orange that she was to unpeel from his mouth. He just had her shove it in for him to unpeel/ eat. They had a lot of fun.

Wednesday morning, Ryanna and Hanna flew to their six week assignment in Bagabag, which is our northern Bible translation center, where she was to help in the school. We were trying to decide with Randall what to do for old time sake, since he was there. Go to the beach, to the mountains, to Bagabag or Nasuli. That afternoon, another man was in the living room of the guest house. We knew him, Randall did not. He was there to pick up a singing group to bring up north, but that fell through and he was going to drive by himself eight hours at night to return to Bagabag. Randall thought that maybe he would welcome a companion to keep him awake, so he volunteered.

When the girls left, Randall and Ryanna exchanged email addresses and said, "Let's keep in touch," which sometimes happens, but often does not. So when Ryanna came out of her house the next day at lunchtime and saw Randall, imagine her surprise! Randall got up, not having any idea where to find Ryanna, but went to the computer department to see if there was anything he could do to lend a hand. It so happened that they were going to dig cable and he volunteered to help. So, there he was, outside of HER house digging cable. She was shocked and hardly said anything, kind of wondering, either he likes me or I'm being stalked!

Meanwhile, back in Manila, we started getting messages from people coming through that our son was being seen "walking the airstrip" which in missionary code means, dating. In a small community with little space to get away to visit, walking the airstrip is it. I'm kind of naïve, so it still didn't register with me that something was going on, but Dave did.

When Randall returned from Bagabag a few days later, I told him that I was going to get a chance to visit with Ryanna's mom when I got home. I had asked her if there were things she didn't want to continue traveling with that I could take home for her, and there were. He responded that he thought that it would be a good idea to see her. I thought, "What?"

THEN, it became clear, that they were starting up a relationship. He made a call home to her dad to ask permission to court his daughter. The funny part is that over the next few days, he wrote back answers three times to her father's inquiries about Randall's intentions with his daughter. He said, "Doesn't he trust me?" I told him, "What a blessing that her dad was protecting her for you."

Later we heard that during this year of travel that Ryanna and Hanna were doing, Hanna was teasing Ryanna that God was going to have her meet a husband on their travels, to which they joked, "yeah, right." When Randall walked in at dinner that first night, Hanna nearly choked! And later talking to them, it turned out that Ryanna kicked her under the table. Who would ever have thought! They lived only three miles away from each other in Dallas but met ten thousand miles away in Manila.

Before leaving the Philippines six weeks later, Ryanna travelled from the Philippines to Indonesia to spend five days at the ministry where Randall was working. They also talked long hours each night by Skype while apart, and the more they learned, the more they knew that this was a match made by God – His good gift to them to find each other.

Let's go back to a year earlier. We've prayed throughout all of our children's lives for God's best choice for spouses for them. Randall knew a year in advance, before finishing his assignment in Bandung, that he would be coming home for Christmas that year. He let his siblings know so that all would be gathered at the same time. Before coming, he told his director that this was his last year at the mission; he would finish in June at the end of the school year.

While he was home for Christmas, a massive tsunami took place in Asia. The place on the beach in Thailand where he had spent the previous Christmas was in the area that was completely destroyed. When he returned to Bandung after Christmas, he took a group of high school students to help with relief work in Banda, Aceh, Indonesia. He learned that they were all very helpful since they spoke the language. Many relief workers could only be helpful to a certain extent, without the language. Randall was fluent in Bahasa Indonesian. Returning to the school, he realized that he could not just return to the US when the skills he had were really needed there in the relief work. When he headed to Aceh after the school year was over, he did not know WHERE he would be working, only that God was leading him to do so. One of the reasons he wanted to return to the States was to look for a wife. As his mom, I reminded the Lord that surely Randall didn't need to come to the States to find a wife; God could send one there!

Imagine MY surprise when God sent this special woman to the Philippines, not Indonesia. God is so full of surprises.

When Randall and his friend, Stephen, were finished with their assignments with Samaritan's Purse, they traveled though Asia, alone and off the beaten path. Much of the time they where there were no Westerners. There were two weeks during which they planned to travel through China and Laos, and they arranged for both of their girlfriends to travel with them during that leg of their journey. What a season of dating! We received a picture of Randall and Ryanna riding an elephant together in Laos and we thought, "Isn't that what people do after they are married?" The world is surely different for our kids.

Randall returned from his missionary work on November 29, 2006. The day after he returned, the people from the computer company where he interned in college called him. They had followed his journeys and knew he was back. So they offered him a job, which he gratefully accepted. With job in hand, he wasted no time proposing and on Christmas Eve at our home, she said, "yes!"

We Praise and Thank God for the loving way in which He shows Himself faithful to bless us with the desires of our hearts!

Psalm 37:4 ASV: Delight thyself also in Jehovah; And he will give thee the desires of thy heart.

Onto a Moving Train

We were at our Southern-most translation center in the Philippines on Mindanao waiting for some friends to arrive at our small airstrip. We had arrived a day earlier. A group of 300 of our colleagues were gathering for our biennial conference. After we said hello to our friend, I introduced myself to Joy who was one of the other passengers on the flight. She said, "Oh, you're Barb Knutson. I'm supposed to say Hi to you from some mutual friends, the Dennises in Taiwan. This was six months after we had arrived in the Philippines, and this touch from home brought on some tears of homesickness.

The Dennises had a big impact on our lives. They were the first "real" missionaries we had known. They stayed with us and we saw that they were just normal folks like us who were willing to make some sacrifices to obey God's call on their lives. They were a joyful and intact family. Something was very doable about that; it was not impossible. God had already been drawing our hearts into missions.

Six months after meeting her, Joy invited me to travel with her and another friend to where she had worked before in Taiwan. They would travel in the summer. I loved the idea but couldn't imagine how I could do that with the responsibility I had to my family.

A short while later, those translators from Taiwan were visiting in Manila and they also invited me to come there to visit. It was easy for them to just leave, since they were all single. But I wondered now that I'd been invited again whether God may have a reason for me to go there. I had not asked Him, I was only looking at this from a human perspective. So I said, "Lord, do you have a purpose for me to go to Taiwan? If so, I'm more than willing, but I'll need for You to confirm this so I know for sure."

Dave and I prayed about it and then waited. We asked our prayer team to pray about this also and they joined us. Over the next two weeks we had two confirmations. One was a letter from our other friends, the Dennises inviting us to come visit them if we ever came to Taiwan. Within the next couple of weeks we started to receive the money that is a necessary aspect of any of our ministry goals. We ordered the ticket. God was guiding and I was going to get a break from my regular role and duties. I was tired and this was a gift from God.

At this time we needed to move out of the home we were in and we figured that surely we would be well settled into our next home before it was time for my trip. Nothing was working out. Two different houses fell through our hands and later we found that one of those had been severely flooded and the other robbed, and we were spared both of those. But the wait was unsettling and we had to keep trusting that God would lead us to the right house for us. When it was time for the other family to arrive, we still had no house. A family of seven with no place to call home! We were convinced that God, in His love, would show us His love in whatever way was His best plan. We had to move back into the guest house. We knew that if we were not settled I'd have to cancel my trip and it was only ten days away. Dave was convinced that God's leading was clear that I should go.

The first morning we were in Taipei, I came down to a late breakfast and said that I thought I'd be a spiritual giant if I had that much quiet time each day! This was a rare luxury for me that they could start to understand. We visited museums and Joy used her little bit of Chinese to get us around. English was not anywhere on signs, one could not get by at all in English back then.

We then boarded a train that was to take us from the north along the eastern coast to the southern point where we would catch a small plane to go to another island. The train stopped half way down the coast and everyone else left. After a while, the conductor came and told us we had to get off. I stayed with the bags while the others headed down the long ramp to the station. They hurried back and said we would all have to go inside, so we hauled all the bags down with us, including the normal "book bag" that always goes along to translation projects. While the others stood trying to decide what to do, I approached the counter and told the agent "Taitung." He tossed his hands in the air, in shock that we would even be considering still going on that train. He pointed to his watch and wrote down 3:15 which was four minutes away. Joy came over and said the Chinese word "three" and we grabbed our tickets. Snatching our bags we returned to the gate which was now locked. We got the attention of the guard who had locked it, he quickly unlocked, and we raced furiously, periodically shifting the extra bag of books between us. We arrived at the platform just as the train was leaving. Somehow, we lifted the suitcases up into the car, then I pushed from the rear to help the other two on, before jumping on the moving train myself! We felt shear awe that God would allow us to make it against all odds. Now there is a high speed train that travels at 300 KPH. I don't suppose that I'd be jumping onto that while it was moving.

The Dennises had met three trains before ours and were wondering if they should just give up. This was before the days of cell phones. Later, I attended their church and we had a lovely visit catching up on our families and ministries. After that I hopped sideways onto the back of his motorcycle, since I was wearing a skirt, and we headed off to the hospital to "do rounds." He talked to me as if I understood all the medical things he was describing, and I have to admit that it really was fascinating so I pretended to understand. The patient I remember the most had been bitten by a snake on his hand. To repair his skin, his hand was grafted to his stomach skin. Once the skin had grown over the area of his hand that was missing, it could be removed from the stomach and sewn back together. Amazing!

Then we took the small plane across to the island and checked into a hotel near the airport. The next day we would travel around the island by motor-cycle. The translators were on the other end of the island. Only one of us knew how to drive a motor-cycle so Joy would take one of us on the back and shuttle ahead while the other walked, then drop off and return to shuttle the next while the other walked. It was quite funny, but it's how you make things work sometimes. After a bit of this I got to thinking, "How hard can it be to drive one of these?" I got on the bike and said, "I can do all things through Christ who strengthens me!" And I took off. We rented another at the next town and from then on it was much easier to get around.

The island had one main road around the perim-eter and the scenery was gorgeous. I ended up taking several trips alone all the way around the island, claiming this territory for God and His purposes.

We had interesting times with the translators, watching them at work, and I also attended a lit-eracy class for women. We visited many in their homes. The culture was very different and these

Bible translators were living here among them only for the purpose of translating the Book of Books into their language. This was quite a challenge and these women were doing well.

The second night we were preparing to leave the translators' home to return to our hotel when one of the missionaries asked if I'd stay behind for a while to have a private talk about some things. I said, "Yes." But saying so meant other things. I had just learned how to ride the bike that day. And I had only been to the hotel one time quickly, so I'd have to find it again in the dark on the other end of the island, alone. Listening to hurting people and caring about them and taking their hurts to the Father was what I love to do most. Here they were in the middle of this place with no other white faces to understand; of course I'd stay.

We stayed up late and she poured out her heart, trusting me with her pains, hurts and disappointments. I could relate to much of her trouble as it was similar in ways to my own hurts and I had been working through my own issues in life.

The next night was to be our last one on the island. I longed to be able to visit more with this friend and bring more encouragement. Since we were leaving in the morning, we had to return our bikes in the late afternoon so we said our goodbyes, knowing there was more to talk about but no time.

I didn't sleep well that night. I knew that I could minister to her and here we were so close, but too far. I knew that Jesus could heal the hurts that I so badly wanted to walk with her through. Even though God doesn't need to use people, sometimes a human touch does help.

We went to the airport at 8 AM. My friend couldn't even see us off as her bad back didn't allow her to ride a bike across to the other side of the island. The plane was delayed due to a storm. The hours came and went. A nice Japanese traveler offered us some of his beer nuts as we hadn't had any breakfast. We passed on the beer.

Hour after hour of waiting patiently, I was plugged in to listen to peaceful music on my walkman. The song, "Here I am, wholly available. As for me I will serve You, Lord" really touched me. It was now 12:30 PM and God was giving my heart instruction. "Go back and minister and help her through her pain." So it was no surprise when one half hour later we were told that the airport was closing for the day because of a typhoon. Come back tomorrow.

"All right, Lord. I'll go. This must be why You sent me here." I was thinking about the John Denver song, "Why me, Lord?" "I can show someone else what I've been through myself on my way back to You."

I had shared with the others what I believed God was telling me to do, they prayed for me as I headed across the island for the night. They were going across the street to the hotel. For the first time in my life I had to think about the essentials that I needed from my suitcase for the night. I took a toothbrush and change of underwear (I already had a small Bible in my purse). Our suitcases were left behind at the airport. It was pouring rain and I was getting cold feet. "What if my friend didn't want to talk about her problems anymore? What if they didn't want me to stay overnight? Oh, Lord, I feel so inadequate for the task." I was about to decide not to go when Joy came back and confirmed that God had led. Again, their prayers and encouragement gave me the strength to press on.

The bus that came by turned out to be the last one of the day to circle the island. There would be no turning back. I hopped aboard, said the name of the village and held out my handful of coins for the conductor to collect the fee. This was a feeling of freedom and total dependence on my Lord.

By the time I arrived, my friend was just finishing at her office for the day. A while later, we returned to her home and were able to spend a long time talking. She was glad that I came back and marveled that God loved her so much that He would send a storm to keep us there so I could come to her. We talked and prayed for hours and experienced the Lords presence in a precious and comforting way.

I left the next morning and marveled at all the ways that God had worked so that He had allowed me to minister in this way to my sister in Christ. She said that a few weeks earlier she had been praying that God would allow us time to talk together. She didn't know that at that time I was nearly cancelling the trip. God is Sovereign. He wants to bless us in so many ways.

There's even more to the story. Because we were delayed on the island, we were not able to spend one more night with my friends, the Dennises. But, we ended up (unbeknownst to us ahead of time) at the same Guest House in Taipei. Sunday morning I was in the living room getting directions written down in Chinese to get to and from church and the Guest House. The Dennises appeared to our surprise and they decided they would accompany me to the church. We were all so glad because at the church there was a time to break up into small groups to pray and this was our only chance to do so. After church we had a quick bite to eat and then we all headed off to catch planes.

The next day after arriving back in Manila, Dave and I found our home that would be our home the rest of our time in the Philippines.

Proverbs 16:33 ASV: The lot is cast into the lap; But the whole disposing thereof is of Jehovah.

Sumatra Believers

After Randall was in Indonesia for about three and a half years he called on a Sunday afternoon. He was so excited. He said, "Mom, when I first came to Indonesia I never in my wildest dreams would have imagined that I would be having the experience I had today." Randall made the trek by motorcycle alone from the south end of the island to the north to be working in the recovery effort after a tsunami. The efforts of the Christians to help with the rebuilding of both livelihood projects and homes spoke volumes to the people. The people asked why they would leave their own families and spend their own money to come to help them. Randall shared that his motivation for being there was because of his love for Jesus and His command to love others with that same love; they started to believe the Gospel. This Sunday what precipitated Randall's call was, he had just been to a worship service with about 50 Sumatran Indonesian Christians. God used the "storms" in many ways, surely this broke down the barriers.

John 13:34-35 ASV: A new commandment I give unto you, that ye love one another; even as I have loved you, that ye also love one another. By this shall all men know that ye are my disciples, if ye have love one to another.

Christmas Miracle – L OVE

I became a "motorcycle momma" when my daughter had the need to borrow my car for work and school, her college car was no longer dependable. Dave and I were shuttling each other back and forth to work. We both worked in the same office but had very different schedules. I decided to get a scooter to ride to work. To make a long story short, when I took my safety course, the scooter they had was not working so I learned to ride on a motorcycle instead.

I didn't know that I was going to LOVE riding – God knew and surprised me with this new area of joy in my life. And with the generous blessing of two friends who helped me buy the motorcycle that another friend sold me, this was a rich blessing.

A year later, another friend had been telling me that he was thinking of selling his bigger bike since he found he wasn't riding it – "just six times in two years," he said. I told him that if he was ever serious about selling it to let me know, as Dave and I would love to ride together. Of course, this would be by faith since we didn't have any more money this time than we had the first time. (We walk by faith and not by sight.) We arranged that over Christmas break I would come out and give it a try.

I took a cool but still lovely ride into the country to see it. I was intending to just get on it and get an idea if I could handle a 650 instead of my 250. I knew I was not in a position to buy it. On the ride over I committed the whole idea to God, not wanting to be foolish to buy something or fall in love with something that was not smart (dangerous) for me. "Lord, I just want to know Your will regarding this. If you mean for me to have it, I know you will make a way, but please just show me if I should pursue this or let the idea go." (He tells us to ask for wisdom and He will give it.)

I hadn't even gotten on the bike yet, and my friend was questioning our missionary support. "You depend on God to provide all you need, right?" "You don't get any paycheck, right?" Yes, to both – for 24 years we had our needs met by God through people who are led by Him to support our work. He said, "Then I want you to have this bike. It's a beauty and needs someone to be lovingly riding it!" Can you imagine my surprise!! We have seen the generosity of God's people in sharing with us for 24 years so we can serve Him. But, this was not a NEED. Most of our support comes from individuals who I consider give like the widow's mite. They don't have lots of money, but yearn to see God's Word in the languages of His children and thus sacrificially support us. And it takes a big team of people like that.

What was so special was the delight with which this friend shared! He was at least as excited about *Giving* as I was about *Receiving*! It was a joyous moment there in his kitchen when we joined together to praise God for this opportunity to glorify Him by sharing in what He wants us to do – to Love one another! I just don't get to experience that very often and thought it was worth sharing with you!

This reminds me of a song that I love and haven't sung for quite a long time I think this is much like how the first century Christians lived:

Let him who has two, give to him who has none.
For of all His commandments, the greatest is love.
Let's share all things common as each man has need,
And then the free gift of Jesus, the nations will see.

Chorus: *Through our love, they can see that He lives.*
The love we receive is the love we can give.
Through our love, they can see that He lives
Jesus has risen, Hallelujah He lives!

The Highlight of our Summer!

W hile visiting friends in northern Minnesota, we stopped to see some old neighbors who were now retired and had moved out to a lake home.

Only the husband was home that morning and we almost left without seeing him. After several knocks brought no response, we called down to the lake and found him working on a plumbing pipe that goes from the lake to his house. We had a wet hug greeting, mutually glad to see each other after many years.

We waited on his dock while he finished his project before heading uphill to the house. Coffee time at his house was always delicious as his wife cooks up healthy luscious treats. We had bran muffins, true to her reputation.

We got quickly beyond "how's it going" to how things were really going in our lives. As good friends, we didn't need a lot of small talk, we really did want to know. And things were not going too well for this friend in his 'golden years'. Several setbacks had led to his retirement years being invested in new and creative ways. He was full of hurt, having been led astray in some business dealings.

We listened and cared and he talked about all the hard stuff, the pain of trust being disappointed and how life doesn't end up going the way we hope it will, even when we plan carefully. The sadness of the relationships that we hope will bring us the most joy sometimes end up empty and hurtful.

We had just returned from our first term as missionaries where we also experienced our own set of difficulties. Through these we also learned more and more of the care and love of God when life is the hardest. Our own needs and desires had become impossible, and for the most part were out of our hands to control. We had come to know that our desires had to become the same as Jesus, to commit to serve Him in love, and trust Him to provide for us as He would. Trusting in His loving character and plan had become for us something we couldn't see ahead of time, but we could trust through faith based on His past proven goodness and hope in the future. We know that God loves us and cares.

As our lives belong to God, He had indeed given us great joy in serving Him, so whether doing so here in the States or in our beloved Philippines, our goal was the same. And His joy filled our hearts with purpose and worth. Our work was often with great pain and difficult circumstances, but what is totally impossible for man only begins what is God's to do, and to show His glory! We live this way most of the time and it is wonderfully joyful that He would call us to live this way.

Back when we were neighbors, we often shared our love for Jesus with this man. Jesus was just becoming real to us at that time and we wanted to share this excitement with him and everyone else. He listened but pretty much told us he had no need for religion in his life. Now we came to talk with him and love him, not to preach at him. We had prayed for him many times over the years.

After a couple of hours of mutually loving one another, he made the statement, "I sure wish I had peace in my life like you do. You seem so fulfilled and enjoy your work so." That was the opening! I said, "You know it's the Lord." That allowed him the opening to share about all the ways he'd been hurt and even cheated by "church people." We know that people will disappoint us, but this is not about church or people, but about a relationship with Jesus. We explained the Gospel to him, about why Jesus died in our place, that we are all guilty and deserve death but because of God's love, Jesus paid the penalty we deserved for our sins.

After further discussion, he finally said, "I've never understood these things quite like that before." This all made sense and he felt loved. We were experiencing God's presence and Dave and I love ministering together like this, using our different gifts together. He said, "Will you pray for me?" We said that we'd been praying for him for many years, "how about this time YOU pray?" He said that he didn't know how, so we assured him that we'd help. He reached out to hold hands around the table and he repeated Dave's words after him, asking Jesus to come into his life and be his Lord and Savior. We all rested in holy hush after the prayer was complete to soak in the presence of God some more. Finally, he broke the silence by saying, "I feel so at peace! The burden I carried before we prayed is completely gone."

Our joy is great as we rejoice with the angels in heaven over this one dear sinner who's come home. For seventy years he had resisted the Gospel, and now he is our brother in Christ.

To God be the glory, great things He has done!

Romans 5:1-2 ASV: Being therefore justified by faith, we have peace with God through our Lord Jesus Christ; through whom also we have had our access by faith into this grace wherein we stand; and we rejoice in hope of the glory of God.

Count Your Blessings

I woke up feeling the blues this morning and so decided to count my blessings instead of thinking of my woes.

In one lifetime I have:

    Walked where Jesus walked

    Taken a first century boat across the Sea of Galilee

    Ridden on an elephant

    Flown in a helicopter and several small planes

    Kissed a grandbaby

    Written a few books

    Caught a 40 pound fish

    Jumped off a waterfall

    Prayed with hundreds of people

    Shared the Gospel and prayed with people to receive Jesus

    Snorkeled in the Atlantic, Pacific and several seas

    Climbed water towers

    Cross-country skied

Downhill skied
Played leading roles in plays
Sang at a couple of friends weddings
Reverse bungee-jumped
Ridden a motorcycle in Myanmar, Taiwan, the Philippines
Home schooled
Sat in hundreds of bleachers at little league games
Done dozens of jigsaw puzzles
Done hundreds of Sudoku puzzles
Raised five wonderful children
Learned to square and round dance
Sang in multiple choirs
Ironed hundreds of my husband's shirts to show him I love him
Taught with an interpreter
Danced at the funeral of a best friend who's now walking streets of gold
Sailed, parasailed and wind surfed
Been on a houseboat trip on Rainy Lake
Won ribbons at a horseshow
Ridden horses on trails
Been on hay rides
Taken the Mississippi Queen paddleboat
Canoed the Boundary Waters
Watched bears eat out of a trash bin
Seen President Bush and had breakfast with Mother Theresa
Visited the Smithsonians

Seen several double and a couple of triple rainbows

Seen a complete circle rainbow

Rejoiced at the graduation of 5 children from High School

Rejoiced at the graduation of 3 children from College

Rejoiced at the graduation of one child from his Master's program

Been in the same prayer group for eight years and seen multiple answers to prayer

Planned events for hundreds of people and fed them

Snowmobiled

Ice fished

Camped out under the stars

Seen dolphins, whales, eagles, armadillos, rattlesnakes

Traveled to Mexico, Canada, and 49 of the 50 United States

Gone on a cruise with the whole family

Traveled to Israel, Egypt, Jordan, Lebanon, Syria, Germany

Traveled to Philippines, Indonesia, Bali, Thailand, Taiwan, Myanmar, Laos, Peru, Malaysia

Learned to sew, knit, crochet, embroider and cross-stitch

Been married to one husband for 33 years

Owned three homes and slept in hundreds of beds

Stayed with friends all over the US and the world

Bubbled in hot springs

Walked in ice water

Been a friend, have lots of friends

Belonged to a tennis league

Been in multiple small groups

Delivered babies

Gone grouse hunting and deer hunting

Shot grouse, watched deer graze

Eaten venison, elk, bear, bison, rattlesnake, coon, squirrel and rabbit

Driven the Blue Ridge Parkway and Natchez Trace

Been a camp counselor and done lots of camping

Been to Machu Picchu and Petra

Hiked lots of wooded trails, mountain passes and sandy beaches

Been to ruins of the Mayan, Inca and Aztec

Been to Holocaust museums in Washington DC and Israel, Gold and Arms museums in Peru, Museum of Science and Industry in Chicago, Masada, Megiddo, Elait, Tiberius and Shrine of the Book Museums in Israel

Supported Jewish people returning to Israel from Eastern Europe

Floated in the Dead Sea and the Great Salt Lake

Ate fudge and rode horseback on Mackinac Island

Ate beniots in New Orleans

Swung in a hammock on South Padre Island at Parrot Eyes

Been to Yellowstone, Mount Rushmore, Grand Tetons, Rocky Mountains,

Olympic National Park, Grand Canyon, Mammoth Cave,

Smithsonian's in Washington DC and Ford theatre,

Mount Vernon and Jamestown, Williamsburg

Been to lots of shows in Branson

Been financially supported by friends and churches in ministry for 26 years

Psalm 103:2 ASV: Bless Jehovah, O my soul, And forget not all his benefits.

Donor Car

When we were preparing to return from the Philippines for furlough, we started praying about a car for our use while back in the States. Only being back for one year we did not want to have a major investment, but we would be traveling a lot of miles visiting many people across the USA, so we would want to have a dependable car big enough for our family of seven to travel comfortably.

Wycliffe had a car donor program where people could donate their cars for just such as us and get a tax deduction also. We were hoping that one would be available, but that isn't always the case.

While in LA, we had some special fun with my sister and nephew and took in Disneyland. We visited our regional office and spent time with other good friends. During our time there, a nice blue Olds station wagon came in and they said that it was ours for the taking. We walked around it, praying, debating. It would mean that we'd have to drive it to Dallas instead of flying. It was tempting. We looked at the tires, good tires! That mattered to Dave; he thought at least we'd have to replace tires on a donated car. Then we looked inside and it had a Craig stereo system. That was the clincher for us. While in the Philippines I had been secretly praying that whatever car we ended up with would have a good stereo since we love to listen to music and stories when we cover all those miles with the children. This appeared to be God's choice.

The next morning Nicole, Valerie and I continued our scheduled flight to Dallas. The boys wrapped up the paper work on the car and secured insurance. They then spent the next three days via the Grand Canyon heading to Dallas with a car they knew nothing about. Thankfully, it was an excellent car and they travelled hassle free. How we thank Jesus for those who are so generous to give like this.

Proverbs 3:9-10 ASV: Honor Jehovah with thy substance, And with the first-fruits of all thine increase: So shall thy barns be filled with plenty, And thy vats shall overflow with new wine.

Don't Sweat the Small Stuff

After living in another culture for a long time, things that used to be annoying take on a new perspective. I was standing in line at the grocery store the other day and the checker was doing her job and also that of the bagger. It was morning and there were not many customers. The lady in line behind me started complaining that she comes to shop in the morning to avoid the crowds but then she has to wait because they don't have enough people working and she has to wait while the checker bags the groceries. How maddening. I heard her through her speech two times then prayed a quick, "Lord, how can I see this in the right perspective" prayer.

I said, "You know, after the way I've shopped the past four years, this is very easy. Even if I had to bag it myself, it's still way easier than having to push to the front of the line to get waited on and then wait while the clerk brought my money across the room to the cashier before returning with my change, several minutes later." The ease of shopping is another one of those things that I won't take for granted here. I also remember the strangeness of the first time the checker asked me "paper or plastic?" That was out of the blue for me, not familiar and I had to ask her to repeat again before asking her what that means.

Proverbs 23:7 ASV: For as he thinketh within himself, so is he.

Leadership Prayer

As I've been more and more put into leader-ship situations, it is becoming clear to me the amount of power there is in this life to influence people. That is so humbling. My heart cry to God is "Please let me use that influence for good ONLY and not to do evil." The temptation to pride, arrogance and all the other pitfalls are all there now which I didn't have to worry about as a homemaker/wife/mother. But how I influence others I desire to come only from God's leading as Lord of my life and then I also want the Glory to ONLY be Gods as well. Loving people is such a privilege. Most of the time it is encouraging and lights become brighter. But sometimes, the message is one of "reproof, correction and training in righteousness" and is not always met with joy. In fact, I remember that it is possible that even doing the right thing will cause one to be "hated for Jesus' sake." But I also know we are warned that in the world we will have "trouble" but that we can stay "in good cheer" since Jesus promised that He has overcome the world. That means for us to be able to do His work in His strength, with peace and joy and love. The whole package! It's not about ME, it's about HIM!!! *Be glorified in my life, Lord. You asked us to Love one another, so show me how to do that.*

John 3:30 ASV: He must increase, but I must decrease.

My New Job after Being Mommy

While my children were still in school, I was working at our mission clinic. Then the Lord was nudging me in a serious way to home-school our youngest three children. I told the Doctor that I would get my kids onto a schedule with their schooling and then let him know when I would be available to help in the clinic. He laughed, which I surely didn't understand at the time. The reality, though, was that his wife had home-schooled their children and he knew more than I the time commitment it would take. He knew I wouldn't be returning anytime soon.

After three wonderful years of home teaching, and with a good new schooling option, I started praying about where I would fit into the work of the mission that we had committed our lives to so many years earlier. I was finishing up my home-schooling years and our kids were all off to school, so I was expecting that I would now be free to become more active in the work than I had been in the past.

At the beginning, we had kids on various schedules at several different schools, so the first year back I was a mommy-chauffeur. Our pace increased over the next several years.

We had been surrendering anew to God, willing to go wherever He wanted us to go, whether in the States, or again to an overseas assignment. We were willing to go or stay, and do His will. Nothing was clear for a while, and we had season of testing our patience. How would we know? "Lord, we trust You."

At one point we were visiting with our Dallas Center Director, just casually shooting the breeze and he was describing some help he needed in a few areas. Since we were leaning toward returning overseas, we were not looking hard here in the States for what we should do next. But, all of a sudden he started describing a person he needed as his assistant. One with good background knowledge of all the work of our mission and its complicated systems. One who could help make budget decisions and work with departments to make upgrades to help things run smoother in all areas. Dave and I both had one of those "Know that you know" moments. We looked at each other with the, "Do you suppose that God is leading us to work here?" look. For Dave, that is. But then, he went on to describe another part of the work that needed lots of coordinating with department managers to find out what is working in different areas and how we could help with other needs. Also he wanted to take the coordination of meeting details off his plate. We both could hardly believe it. He was now describing my passions and gifts. So, together he was describing both of our areas that we know, we love, and are gifted to do. We asked him whether he could be describing a shared position for us. And that's how we both took on new roles as Assistant Director (me) and Associate Director (Dave) of the Dallas Center which hosts our International Administration and our training school for Bible Translators.

I had been a homemaker. I knew that I had various skills. I raised a large family, moving them back and forth across the ocean with all the details that go into all the implications of that. I reared the children to be self-starters, and to have all five gain scholarships so they could attend college. So I must have some skills. But, could I really handle the full time work environment? In an office?

My First Day on the Job

I arrived first thing in the morning and since Dave actually started the day before I did, he already knew what he was doing. So I met in the Directors' office for the first couple of hours to get my marching orders. One of the things he told me then was that I was starting with a borrowed desk chair as mine was still on order. He left a note on the man's desk that if he came back before his chair did, to come and get it. I was just leaving the Director's office when Sam came by to wheel his chair out. Dave jokingly grabbed our Director's chair and teased, "Well, we'll have to find her one." Then he let it go. But this servant leader grabbed his chair and said, "Yes, that's right" and proceeded to move his chair into my office.

We worked it out to find another one so we all ended up with chairs, but his movement to give me <u>his</u> chair spoke volumes to me of his servant leadership, the kind I'd need as I began in something as big as this new role. I knew from that moment that I was going to love working for this boss.

I learned from a Ken Blanchard manager development meeting that one of the marks of a real leader is that his employees are proud to be associated with him. And they want to work hard and help the leader be successful. That's true.

Colossians 3:23 ASV: whatsoever ye do, work heartily, as unto the Lord, and not unto men;

Eccelsiastes 3:22 ASV: Wherefore I saw that there is nothing better, than that a man should rejoice in his works; for that is his portion: for who shall bring him [back] to see what shall be after him?

Tough Challenge

Before we headed overseas for our first missionary assignment, Wycliffe had a pre-field training course called "Jungle Camp." Ours was held in a remote location in the desert of Southwest Texas near a town called Uvalde. There were lots of difficult things they did to try to help us prepare for the cross-cultural challenges we would be facing. They turned off the electricity sometimes to see how we'd cope, and one time after returning from a long hike they turned the water off.

We learned to give each other shots and also learned how to tie stitches on pigs feet. This was all supposed to be kept secret from one group to the next so that everything would catch us by surprise like most cultural challenges. One thing that we had gotten wind of ahead of time was that each of us would be required to butcher a chicken. To me that was about the most horrible thing I could imagine to do in the entire world.

The day came and the leader showed us a method to make the chicken dizzy by twirling it in the air. Then he put it under a broomstick and pulled the feet to pop the head off. After that, a Nebraska farm lady, one of the students in training, showed us how to put that dizzy chicken on a stump and do the dirty deed with an ax. All the while I was having this talk with Jesus, taking my fears to Him. My whole body was reeling from the emotional attack. I remember thinking, "Lord, help me to do this quickly and get it over with. If I don't just get up there and do it immediately, I feel like I'll turn and run and maybe not stop till I hit Mexico."

I was the first to volunteer and thought that the broomstick method was the more humane for me. So I swung her around and lay the broomstick over her neck and planted both feet on either side of the stick. And then I pulled and pulled some more. And the neck kept stretching and stretching until this delirious bird popped right out from under the stick and crazily made its way into the bushes. The whole group stopped to watch while I gathered it again, since I still had to kill it, and was told there was only one bird for each person and this was mine. I got the stick all prepared again and this time realized from everyone's directions that the idea was to "pop" the head from under the stick. I did that and was successful. One of the instructors took pictures of my horrified, expressive face. I asked him afterwards for the pictures so I could destroy them.

That night we also were told that our assignment was to "cook" our birds over an open fire as family units. We had a bland diet day after day, always the same, so the thought of great chicken pieces sounded wonderful to us. We cut it up and cooked it golden brown and it looked lovely. But then, as we each tried to take a bite, we were startled to not even be able to break the skin. We didn't know that these were old birds and very tough. So, another lesson the Nebraska farm girl didn't need to learn the hard way as she boiled hers in a pot for a long time to make it tender. We did that the next night as we ended up cooking outdoors for the week.

Over the years there have been so many times when life was "hard." God was asking us to do things that were stretching our faith and to obey meant to have to suffer the challenge to obey. Each time it all seemed impossible, one of us could say, "remember the chicken." If I was able to do that, there is nothing I can't do.

Philippians 4:13 ASV: I can do all things in him that strengtheneth me.

Valley Verde

We had been in the Philippines for three months, staying in the home of some missionaries who had taken a short furlough. They were due back and we still hadn't secured a home for our family for the remainder of our time in the Philippines. In Sunday school, someone handed us a slip of paper that told us about another missionary family that was going to the States for one year and needed someone to stay in their home. We really didn't want to have to do that and move again in another year. But we were about out of time so we went to see it.

It was actually a long distance away from our mission center which had some pros and cons. The further out we went, we were wondering if we really wanted to be that far away, as traffic was difficult. Just a few blocks from the house, we passed by a country club that we had been to for a birthday party for one of our son's friend. My prayer was, "Lord, if You're going to have us live this far out, it would be nice to belong to the club." The Manila heat is unbearable at times and often there were also power outages and a daily swim was a necessary part of "keeping our cool." Even though swimming at the club seemed like an extravagance for missionaries, our mission pool would be a long ways away.

We decided to take that house and shortly thereafter I contacted the club to find out what it would cost us to join. It was too extravagant for our budget.

From the beginning of our training with Wycliffe I was aware that there would be a lot of cultural things that we'd be learning and I was going to need someone who I could come to for advice and help in making it work. I prayed that God would provide this person for us.

A few days after moving in, a neighbor came to visit. She was an American married to a Filipino who had lived in the Philippines for nineteen years. She knew about changing cultures and what I'd need to learn. I realized that she was God's answer to my prayers. She helped with things regarding training house help and doctors and buying replacement gas tanks and things for the house. She was very helpful and encouraging to me.

She also came over one day and said, "Since you are missionaries, I suppose you won't be joining the country club. I want you to know that you are welcome to use our membership at any time. I had dropped the thought and again, God met my desire so clearly to bless us.

We were able to bless and entertain many weary coworkers who needed the relaxing and serene atmosphere away from the Manila stresses. Something else God showed me in my heart, that just because we were missionaries, we were not second-class citizens. We were able to enjoy things as much as anyone else.

Mark 6:30-32 ASV: And the apostles gather themselves together unto Jesus; and they told him all things, whatsoever they had done, and whatsoever they had taught. And he saith unto them, Come ye yourselves apart into a desert place, and rest a while. For there were many coming and going, and they had no leisure so much as to eat. And they went away in the boat to a desert place apart.

Never Give Up

W e were working in Manila. From Dave's desk as the Philippine Branch Finance Director, he often was the first person translators would see when they returned to the city after being out in the village for a long time. The condition of their finances was often a concern. That was where he found out about a lot of needs going on in people's lives and he regularly invited people home for dinner and games with our family. On one such occasion, one of our translators had been working on their translation for six years. Before coming to Manila, he had made up his mind that he had been at this work for too long without any obvious results. Six years he had been learning the language and living among the community. In all that time there was not even one person who was following Jesus. Part of his plan in coming to Manila was to start the process of giving up. He said, "I'm wasting our time, we're wasting our supporters money. Nothing is happening. It's time to quit." Before he left the village, God had a surprise for him.

Part of the early stages of Bible translation includes the rough draft versions of the translation. Rough drafts of the work are printed out and distributed to some in the area who are willing to read it for clarity and help make changes. One young man, Daniel, had been helping in this way. One day, he came to the translator and said, "This is the truth. I want to become a Christian." The translator questioned him, reminding him of the possible rejection from all in his community and the consequences he may face. He still wanted to become a follower of Jesus. The missionary was thinking, "I wonder where I can take him off to baptize him in some quiet private place." Then Daniel said, "It says here that I'm supposed to be baptized as a public witness to the fact that I am now following Jesus."

He wanted to be baptized in the middle of town so all would know of his decision to follow Jesus, whatever the cost to him. Daniel talked this over with his father and he said that whatever he decided, he should do it whole-heartedly. Thereby, he was giving his permission which is quite cultural.

Daniel was obviously gifted and loved to debate in the village square the differences he was now learning as he devoured the Word of God

Sometimes it is hard to wait in the dark when from a human perspective nothing seems to be happening. And all the more now when churches want to "SEE" numbers and results of what the Lord is doing. Some things cannot be measured that way. The virtue in the waiting is a higher calling. God alone knows what His purposes are and sometimes we just have to trust Him and wait. Edith Edman once said, "Never doubt in the dark what God has shown you in the light."

Galatians 6:9 ASV: And let us not be weary in well-doing: for in due season we shall reap, if we faint not.

Ephesians 3:20 ASV: Now unto him that is able to do exceeding abundantly above all that we ask or think, according to the power that worketh in us,

At the Cabin

About six months before we were to return to the USA after being away for four years we started to think about where we would live and set up house for our furlough year. This was our first time and we knew people all over the US, and didn't know how to plan to be in an area long enough for our children's school schedule and still to see everyone.

I wrote to a few prayer partners to ask them to pray about this and see if anyone knew a place where we could stay in the Minneapolis/ St. Paul area. At this same time I was in bed with hepatitis so while sick, I was also making plans for our next several months trying to prepare to leave the Philippines. To our surprise we received an invitation from one of our supporters asking if we'd like to use their summer lake home as our headquarters. What a fantastic gift! We said, "Yes" and every day as we prepared we thanked God for that incredible gift.

The next few months of getting ready were very hard. I was still recuperating from the hepatitis and never got my full energy back the rest of our time there. Dave was busy trying to train the man who had come to replace him. Looking forward to time at the cabin gave us the endurance we needed.

I was picturing the lakes and the trees and the peace and quiet. Our family had been there a few times before we were missionaries. We parked our camper there and spent time with the family at the lake. The anticipation of going "home" was sometimes just so great.

The cabin did bring us much rest and refreshment. From the beginning I knew that the pace would help us to recover from the stresses of living in a very difficult environment. It was quiet and private. We were also delighted for our children to experience some of the beauty of the outdoors in Minnesota that we had enjoyed growing up.

Fishing occupied a great deal of our time. Our three boys had played baseball on an international league in Manila so we looked for and found teams that they could join in Minnesota for the summer.

One day the kids were inside and said, "There's nothing to do." We all sat down at the counter to think about some of the options for fun in the outdoors when they needed an idea. Our list was like this:

Sailing, canoeing, soccer, baseball, biking, fishing, swimming, hiking, play in tree house, croquet, practice shooting bb guns, building, digging, games, puzzles, cards, Frisbee, toys, catching frogs or night crawlers.

We hung this list on the refrigerator and agreed that there should be no reason for anyone to get bored. There were several times during the summer that I saw someone looking for ideas from the list.

The Lord really does give us the desires of our hearts. The quiet of the woods and lake were a significant resting place for us and the sailing was peaceful and re-energizing. Dave was able to catch fish to his heart's desire and we ate all we wanted and still had plenty to feed large crowds that came for a visit, and sent packages home with them also. That's fishing!

Being at the cabin gave our family a place of our own to have guests. Both sets of our parents were able to come up as well as several siblings and their families. Some supporters and even friends from the Philippines made their way over. What a wonderful way to start our time back in our home country.

This has been a stable place for our children to connect and each have at different times made their way back for a week or so.

Psalms 119:165 ASV: Great peace have they that love thy law; And they have no occasion of stumbling.

John 14:27 ASV: Peace I leave with you; my peace I give unto you: not as the world giveth, give I unto you. Let not your heart be troubled, neither let it be fearful.

Wildlife and Poison
in Missions

I remember hearing about a time when one of our Bible translators was working in her village. The way that the Bible Translation process works is that some rough drafts of the Word are translated from the Bible, and then they are tested by several local people to make sure that the meaning comes across culturally correct from the original intent of the message. The translator was working on the book of James. She had several copies passed out into the community for evaluation.

Two little boys (maybe 5 and 7) had been to the forest and eaten poison berries. Their dad was one who had a copy of the book of James to read. Since people were responding SO well to the Scriptures, the translator wanted to get it into their hands ASAP (and they kept asking for more). A few days after he got it he came running, "Come quick, my boys are dying!" Everyone knew that those who ate the berries died. The translator froze. She did lots of medical work (delivered babies, even sutured wounds) but she had NO idea what to do for poison. She was paralyzed. He was increasing in anxiety. "Can't you at least come and pray?! That's what that James you gave me to read says!" She followed, trembling, up the ladder; there were those violently ill little boys. She prayed something and when she looked up, they were completely well! All were awed at God! The dad said, "That's what it said, wasn't it!"

In a village on a lake near a large river in Papua New Guinea, a translator's family lived on a houseboat while they taught literacy to the villagers and completed the first draft of a New Testament. The dad worked with language helpers and the mom home-schooled their two sons on the boat. The climate was hot and mosquitoes almost unbearable, but each day the two boys swam along with village children in the swampy lake. In their bright orange life jackets, they paddled from the houseboat to a small raft anchored a short distance away. The villagers said that the *puk-puks*, the crocodiles, only inhabited the far side of the lake and didn't come over to the village area. That sounded good. When the first draft of the translation was completed, the couple planned to travel in the houseboat on the main river and teach reading. However, during the three years the family lived on the lake, the channel from the lake into the river became totally clogged with an invasive weed. The couple could not travel in the houseboat. The translation still needed to be typed and checked, so the translators wondered what they should do.

While they were on furlough in the States, the villagers hooked and hauled a huge, fifteen foot long croc out of the lake. God had clearly protected the swimmers. This seemed to be confirmation that the family should move to another location to continue to check and prepare the translation for publication. A picturesque rain forest setting was a welcome change from the swamps. And, the pythons in the jungle only lived on the other side of the small stream where the children now played.

Missionaries often encounter poisonous critters of various kinds. There is a well-known but not official way of dealing with the toxins. No one in their right mind would patent this and risk the legal issues. Some missionaries use the common "stun gun" that is sold for women's self-defense as it can be used on various poisons. We've heard of people using this method successfully on venomous snake bites, scorpion bites, red ant bites, spiders and such. A zap from this electric charge will neutralize the protein in the venom. Of course if a hospital and anti-venom are available, that is always the first preferable choice. But if not, this is another good way and worth a try. I've only used it one time myself when a friend was bitten by a black widow spider. She called me at 11 at night and asked if I could come up with a stun gun. I found someone who had one and then went about finding fresh batteries, but we were able to zap her bite within a half an hour and there were no ill effects.

Psalm 23:4 ASV: Yea, thou I walk through the valley of the shadow of death, I will fear no evil; for thou art with me; Thy rod and thy staff, they comfort me.

Light Out of Darkness

One of the ministries that I had at our church was to be available in the Prayer Rooms after the services to pray with anyone who had a need. One man came in who was deeply discouraged. From all outward appearances, he had life all together. He was a successful Dallas business man. Yet, he was revealing to me deep fears and inadequacies.

The prayer room is not a counseling center but sometimes as the Holy Spirit leads there are words that bring a kind of depth and healing when needed. I asked him if he had ever let himself look deep at the flood of fears and weaknesses that were bottled up deep inside. It would look very, very dark. In that darkness is the realization that we are not to carry the weight of the world on our shoulders. We are weak and fearful. With the knowledge of that truth is the realization of our need for light. And Jesus IS the Light. He wants to come in like a FLOOD to the deepest part of our souls to carry our load and shine the light of His love into us. That is what gives us strength and comfort, and then shines through us into the dark world. The world then sees His glory and love shining through us. God's perfect love casts out our fears.

In him was life; and the life was the light of men. 5 And the light shineth in the darkness; and the darkness apprehended it not. John 1:4-5

A Quiver Full and Then Some

Most of our married lives my husband Dave and I have had Bible studies in our home. At one time we had four going on in various forms between us. The current one at this time was a group of about eight or so who had come forward at a crusade meeting in town and expressed an interest in being in a Bible study. None had ever attended one before. We were a new group and after only a couple of weeks, our fourth child was born. We didn't miss a beat, we just went in, had the baby, and were back the same week to meet with our groups.

With our new arrival it brought a discussion of children. There in our group was a mother and her twenty-something son. She made the comment, "Steve here, he's my youngest!"

"Oh, really, how many children do you have?" "Seventeen," said this sweet, calm, pleasant woman.

That night in bed, Dave had a restless night, which meant I did also. He actually kept waking up, sometimes he sat up straight in bed and said out loud, "seventeen." He'd roll over and mumble, "Seventeen."

Psalm 127:3-5 ASV: Lo, children are a heritage of Jehovah; And the fruit of the womb is his reward. As arrows in the hand of a mighty man, So are the children of youth. Happy is the man that hath his quiver full of them: They shall not be put to shame, When they speak with their enemies in the gate.

Valentine Flowers

I was in the "Boutique" which is our other name for the mission barrel, where members of the community bring in their gently used items for distribution among the missionaries. I asked a friend, "When is Valentine's day?" She said, "Tomorrow." On the spot I had an idea that can only have been God-breathed. I started pulling baskets off the top shelves and vases off of others until I had a large pile. Then I hurried to check with my director to see if he'd OK the idea that I was having.

I asked him, "Can I have some fun?" And he said, "Yes." I responded, "Before I even tell you what I'm scheming, you'll say, yes?" We both laughed. It's such a rich blessing to have his vote of confidence like that! I told him that I was thinking about arranging some flowers for the gents around the mission to have available on a donation basis to give to their sweethearts. He liked the idea. It was late morning and I had to go home, get soup to bring to an elderly gentleman and be back by two o'clock for a meeting. That left me just an hour and a half or so to shop for flowers for this wild, off-the-cuff idea.

I dashed to Sam's and having never arranged flowers before, had no idea what quantity I'd need, in fact I had no idea how many containers I had collected. But I knew that besides the flowers, I'd need some greens and baby's breath to make them pretty. I also stopped in to pick up ribbons from the sewing room at the Boutique.

I went to the meeting, came home and washed all the containers, and started putting ribbons on each one while at the same time preparing a Lutefisk dinner for company we were having over for supper. Company stayed until 9 or so and then I went to work, getting some basics ready to go. I knew that I couldn't put them together too much ahead of time or it would be hard to transport them so anything with vases of water had to wait and the baskets had a few basic roses in each. I fitted the wet foam into each basket and lined several laundry baskets with vases and baskets. The flowers were in a large bucket of water. I also talked my friend, Elaine, into showing up the next morning to put them together.

We met at 8 AM at the dining hall, and set the containers on two long tables that we had decorated with red cloth and hearts. One long table held all the loose flowers and we went to town putting more into this or that type of container until, just before all the people arrived at 10 for an all-center meeting, all 80 vases and baskets were complete and looked so beautiful!!! Some were large baskets and others were simple with just a few pretty things. Some people wanted roses and others wanted anything but roses, like lilies, tulips, etc. But all in all, by the time people left the meeting all were snatched up by very happy customers and quite a pile of donations were collected to help missionaries on the center with extra needs. 24 hours and such a blessing!

His Touch

Many years ago, I used to play my guitar and lead worship for small group Bible studies. I sang at a couple of my friends' weddings. But that was something I gave up over the years. The church we attended in the US was so large, you had to be a professional musician to lead.

When asked to be on the leadership team for a ladies retreat, I found the courage to volunteer to lead the worship. I had filled in once at a home Bible study group and had the urge to again sharpen those musical gifts that lay dormant. My fingers still had a degree of callous even after many years of inactivity. So I practiced and prayed for God's leading regarding which songs to use in worship. The weekend came and I was joyful about leading others to worship God. I pictured it being like I worship with abandon in the quiet of my own living room. Now I would just be taking my sisters in Christ along with me.

Friday night came and I pictured showing up, knowing that the power of God's Holy Spirit would take over for any of my own weakness to allow us to "fix our eyes on Jesus" and delight Him in our worship. That was not how it went. I had memory blanks, and repeated some parts of songs at the wrong places. During Communion I was supposed to play "Just As I Am" on the piano. What I hadn't thought of was that the woman who was doing the overheads would be passing out the bread and grape juice. I went looking for the overhead and couldn't find it. Plus I didn't even know how to turn on the overhead. So I proceeded to the piano and played one verse badly, feeling over my head and the frustration of not doing it right.

It was obvious to many that this was not going as we all on the leadership team had hoped. A friend passed me a note and prayed for me before I got in my car. Her note reminded me that God loved me and was delighted with me. He would give me strength and courage. I felt so thankful that she did this, as almost everyone else just left without a word.

Trying to sleep, there were three times I woke up with the deep flush feelings of shame, embarrassment, failure, inadequacy. As those feelings washed over me, I decided not to try to make them go away, but to hold out my pain to Jesus and let Him touch my soul with His love. When I woke in the morning, the feelings of shame were not there. I did think about not going back, but decided that I'd see most of these women again and would have to face them sooner or later, and I had committed to do this, through good or bad. The verse that God gave me to give me courage to return was "We are more than conquerors through Him who loved us." I again committed myself to God and His purposes and the verse, "I can do all things through Christ who strengthens me."

I decided that forty was too many songs to choose from, which added to the confusion so I picked a dozen that I knew I could play. The leadership team met for prayer and some empathized with me, others wanted me to have time with the Lord to fall apart, but the overall hope for the retreat continued to be letting the Lord meet the women wherever we were and touch us. I had the thought that if we were looking for His healing touch, what better example than for my public display for Him to show His power to heal and transform. I thought it would give others hope that if God could move through me in my failure and weakness, they would believe that He could also meet whatever their burden was, and bring them to victory.

The music was much better throughout that day. My first devotion time I was reading in Romans 8 and found there the verse He gave me to start my day, Romans 8:37. I hadn't remembered the reference so this was a surprise and confirmation.

The next quiet time with Him I was reading about the woman who broke the alabaster jar to anoint Jesus. Even though others thought there could have been a better use for it, Jesus told her she had done a beautiful thing and He was very pleased that she gave Him what she could. He was pleased with my efforts.

The other thing God showed me is that in my weakness the other ladies were all singing heartily, worshiping God with all their hearts. I think if I were entertaining, people may have focused on me and not Him.

But we have this treasure in earthen vessels, that the excellence of the power may be of God and not of us. 2 Corinthians 4:7, NKJV

I would prefer to come off singing beautiful. Am I willing to suffer even if I don't understand why so He can accomplish His plans? I say again, *Let it be to me according to your word. Luke 1:38, NKJV*

I received another note on the way out. It said, "I love worship that allows me to smile at and with God. Yours did that well." That's right! Lord, keep me out of the way.

Encouragement

The kids had just been back in school for a week and I was ready to get back to all the unfinished projects that had piled up all summer while I was busy enjoying the kids. Over the weekend, I had the worst flu symptoms ever. I was so weak I couldn't get out of bed and was wracked with pain and nausea. On Monday morning, the light shone in from the window. I looked at my skin and saw a light glow, kind of golden. Could it be what I was guessing?

Dave took me to the doctor to confirm my suspicion of having hepatitis A. The reality of this was sinking in and I was thinking about all that I had to do. We stopped at our mission headquarters before heading home where I was to recuperate for six weeks. I told a friend and she put her arm around me to comfort me. I said to her, "Didn't you hear me, hepatitis?" Like a leper, I couldn't imagine anyone wanting to touch me. She said, "Let's pray." That lifted my spirit so much. My friend had made a commitment to encourage others, and that goal was as big as my need to be loved at that time.

We had attended a seminar all summer on encouragement, by Larry Crabb. He is seriously committed as am I to Hebrews 10:24-25 and how important it is that we "stir one another up to love and good works, not neglecting to meet together but encouraging one another."

We missionaries go to the mission field well-trained in all that is needed to do a top rate job in Bible Translation and that is good. We need also to be prepared for the "One-Anothers" in giving and receiving care and encouragement. It can be very hard sometimes, and good interpersonal relationships can make a difference whether we succeed or not. These skills are just as important as the tools for Bible Translation.

Even we old timers need to look in the mirror and ask the question, "How am I doing at building and encouraging relationships?" I want to grow to be more like Jesus!

Years One, Two, Three, Four

As we progressed through the years of our first missionary term of service, there were many changes that took place as we adjusted to life in another culture. Some of these are familiar to most everyone in the missionary community. Some parts are difficult to adjust to, but others are rich in blessing.

The first year upon arriving is the "Honeymoon" stage, especially for the first-time missionary. "We've finally arrived!" All those years of preparation, what a privilege to finally be where God has called me and is going to use me! The anticipation of all that is ahead is unique; it's new and different and can be kind of fun and adventurous. Having a live-in maid sounds heavenly to one who has always done her own housework. Finding out that the ocean is only a couple of hours away and discovering a world of underwater beauty can counter a bit of stress. I came to the mission field fully confident that "I can do all things through Christ who strengthens me."

Therefore, nothing God, the mission, or anyone else asks will be beyond His grace for me to accomplish. The "rose-colored" glasses were on snugly and securely. We knew things would be different and we'd have to adjust to some things in a culture different from our own. That made sense to us.

What we were blinded to was the pain that was the reality of our experience within our mission culture. Everything seemed wonderful.

Then the second year came. Now it was time for some introspection – *Who am I and what am I here for? What are my expectations? What things from my own culture do I need to hold on to for survival here, and in what can I flex, to adjust and live here? Am I strong in the Lord? What's reality, truth, freedom? What is a missionary? God loves me. Am I to do anything more than survive?*

Year three was, I think, the year I experienced the most culture shock. My rose-colored glasses were shattered. The newness had worn off and we started to ask ourselves, *You mean we really have to live like this? What things in the culture are making me angry? And I'm to "sin not." Help, Lord! Am I running to the Lord and trusting Him for victory in my life?*

Who is the enemy, anyway? I'd run home if I could. Or would that mean that I were running away from God? If I run to God will He really show me how to love those who are hurting me? Somehow I'm to maintain balance and a sane lifestyle while my world is constantly changing. And bear fruit? "For God has not given us a spirit of fear, but of power and of love and of a sound mind." (2 Timothy 1:7, NKJV)

Year four: preparing for furlough brought many new questions to wrestle with: *Do we keep household goods and all the stuff that we've finally accumulated to make it comfortable for us here, or get rid of it and start all over after a year away? What will our loved ones be like after we've been apart for four years – we've changed, have they? What gifts can we bring to our loved ones that show we care, are not junk, but that we can afford and will fit in suitcases? Where to live and where to set up house for one year? Goodbye to friends here, some for two years as our furloughs will overlap. Will you still be my friend? Every year, many friends left and old ones returned. Sometimes people didn't return.*

In each stage, God confirmed that we were meant to be where we were. That's what gave us confidence to courageously face each stage and make it through. To God be the Glory!

Attending a New Testament Dedication

W hat an incredible experience! Going to the New Testament dedication on the island of Caluya was indeed like traveling to a different world. There isn't even one car on the island. It has the most beautiful long white sand beach, sunsets are astounding, the pace of life is a very welcome s-l-o-w. To those of us who love snorkeling, it was some of the best underwater we've seen. About the only thing we really have in common with the Caluyanuns is a love for the Lord Jesus. And in that we enjoyed a terrific time of fellowship.

I was the only female in our travelling group of five. After a smooth and uneventful flight we landed at a private airstrip on a neighboring island.

We then went by open *banca*, which is like a motorized outrigger canoe, along with 4 cows, rice sacks of pigs, and the Bibles to Caluya. Raquel, (who is the translator's wife and Caluyanun) and her many relatives showed Caluyanun hospitality, as we

Westerners were a real novelty. Kermit Titrud, the translator, informed us that he had a surprise for us. All the animals that traveled with us were to become the food for the celebration the next day. Outside our window that night, a couple dozen men would be butchering the meat for the big event the next morning. Talk about fresh meat! So, starting about 10:00 PM, we watched them get started, the cows moaning. After committing the matter of sleep to our loving Father who knew we needed it, we all found that we were able to get a good night's sleep, even though each of us was reminded once or twice during the night of the event by the sounds of chopping or mooing.

The excitement was high as people testified to how eager they were to study God's Book. Pastor Ysug is the son-in-law of the first believer on Caluya. He told of coming to preach after getting his training. He preached first in Togalog, but that didn't communicate. Then he tried Hilongo, another neighboring language, but was growing weary at that. He knew that the only way the Caluyanun people would really understand God's Word and his ministry would go on after he left was for him to translate and preach in Caluyanun. He began the translation work himself. When Kermit did a survey and they found each other, they knew it was a match made in heaven.

The Caluyanun people have a great love for Kermit, and everywhere he went, he has discipled men who now are pastoring several churches, all in the Caluyanun language. We had two more mini-dedications at churches back on another island.

Our return trip was quite eventful, as we were on a smaller open boat and the ocean was pitching. We were all glad that we waited until we arrived to have breakfast. The flight back had its share of bumps, but we know the angels were sitting on the wings to stabilize the plane.

For Dave and me, it was really an encouragement, reminding us of why we were committed to Bible Translation. Sometimes that can get lost as we push a pencil around in Manila. The excitement of the people as they received God's Word in their own language is forever planted in our minds.

The Chief End of Man

Walking with Jesus
Talking with Jesus
Seeing the world through a Biblical perspective
Setting your mind on things above
Knowing His presence
Surrendered to His will

This is the Joyful Christian life

There is no greater joy than that your children walk
in the truth. If that is true for us, how much more
does it bless Our Father when we walk in truth?

Delight yourself in the Lord, and He will give you
the desires of your heart.
I delight to do Your will, O my God, Thy law is
within my heart.

From the Catechism:
"What is the chief end of man?"
To glorify God and to ENJOY Him forever.
Does that mean this is the whole reason we exist?

Motorcycle Help

Driving my motorcycle to our mission center in Dallas is just a few mile ride on back country roads with little or no traffic along a beautiful tree lined, lake in the back ground route. It is always refreshing to my soul to be out in the breeze, enjoying this little time with the Lord. One day I was just a couple of blocks from home. I had my cell phone safely tucked in my "extra purse," my bra, when it vibrated that I had an incoming call. I pulled over to the side of the road to answer the call. I was talking for about 3-4 minutes when I happened to look across the street. There in the yard was an elderly man, maybe 80 years old. He was working on trimming his trees in the Texas heat and had fallen. He was motioning for me to come help him. I quickly hung up the phone and hurried over to him. I got him back into the safety of his home and got him some water and found his favorite chair. Assured that he was all right, I returned to my bike, still parked in the street with the key in the ignition.

My thoughts quickly turned to how much the Father loves us. This man was in need, I don't know if he was calling out to God for help, but he did need help. So God arranged a cell phone call just then, just to help him. Isn't that a loving God? If I'd have just driven by I would never had seen him.

Another time a few years earlier I was riding my cycle to our departmental prayer meeting. On the way, I heard my garage door opener fall out of my pocket and onto the road. I stopped my bike and ran back to get it. Directly across the road was a man with a pickup truck who was standing there leaning on his truck. I called across to him, "are you OK?" He answered that, "no he was not." He had been four wheeling in a field there and run out of gas. He pushed his four-wheeler to the curb where he had parked his pickup. It was a muddy day and from the looks of the tread marks, he had tried unsuccessfully to wheel the vehicle into the back end of the truck up the board ramp. He had no cell phone and he needed gas to be able to get his four-wheeler up the ramp. I decided that I could head home for our gas can, stop by the gas station and get some gas and bring it to him. I returned and he put the gas in and I watched him easily ride his four-wheeler into the truck bed. He asked how he could repay me and I told him that it was just God meeting his need that he had and the best way was to pass it on when he sees a need. He told me that he had been stuck there for at least an hour and I was the first to stop.

I got to my prayer meeting fifteen minutes late and explained my delay. One of the others in my prayer group said that he had seen the stranded man also. Hmm. Maybe sometimes we need to adjust our agendas to meet people needs, don't know for sure, just thinking.

I don't just stop and help everyone on the road who needs help, like with car trouble, I would be of no help, the blind leading the blind. But when God wants me to be available, He adds another element to make it clear that I am to go and help.

Sometimes we may find ourselves helping angels unaware.

Whatever we do to the least of our brothers we do to Him!

Rainy Halloween

On Saturday it was raining cats and dogs when we arrived in Manila and since it was "rainy season" we didn't give it much thought; we just stayed in and rested to recover from jet lag. On Sunday morning we attended one of the Filipino churches we've visited before. I sang a song for them and this is what I sang:

We are pilgrims on a journey, we are brothers on the road.
We are here to help each other walk the mile and bear the load.
When we sing to God in heaven we shall find such harmony.
Born of all we've known together of Christ's love and agony.
*chorus- And we who are many are one body in Christ, in Christ.
And everyone members of one another, loving each other, with God as our Father

Who loves us as a mother loves her little child.
Repeat chorus.

In the afternoon we drove out to San Mateo where we had planned to worship together with this young church, however, they would have no service today. We witnessed devastation from flooding in Manila which had not been seen in fifty years. Instead of worshiping together, the church members were cleaning out mud from their homes, that is, those who were fortunate enough to still have homes. Many homes that had lined the river were in pieces down river. The church meeting hall was full of mud and the bookshelf with the Bibles was tipped on its side, the Bibles ruined. The electric fans and music equipment were all in piles of mud. We did not know that this was coming but God did. There were 18 of our faith support team who had responded the two weeks before to what we called our "Halloween Challenge." We asked people to give what they would normally spend just on Halloween stuff as a love gift to help this young church. We were thinking like for a new podium, or needed equipment.

You can only imagine how blessed the pastor and his wife were when we handed them that substantial gift that was an immediate help in the aftermath of the typhoon that hit them. We arrived in Manila just before the planes were diverted. After that the airport was stalled for the next couple of days. God let us slide in and be able to go there to really be helpful in their time of need.

The pastor called on two other pastors working in that area to buy supplies for the people's immediate needs and to help distribute them. They came by to tell us that they were going to make sure that all the church members were cared for. We suggested that perhaps they might consider giving each church member enough for their neighbors needs also, an idea which they quickly adapted to. When we returned two months later to visit that church it had doubled in size!

Follow Me and I will make you Fishers of Men.

DANGERS

There were only a couple of times in our missionary career when we felt in real danger. Surprisingly, they were not the most obvious times. We lived through a military coup attempt in Manila, watching bombing planes fly overhead. We couldn't go out of our yard for five days, but we were never feeling our lives threatened.

Another time that we should have felt endangered, but were naive enough to not be concerned was when we traveled by a little outrigger canoe in the open ocean, with the tides rising in preparation for the oncoming typhoon a day later. I was sick, yes, but not feeling endangered.

But the two times we did experience fear were both when we trusted the lives of our family to the bus drivers on Mountain roads.

The first time was when we were traveling from the border of Mexico into the capitol city. The trip was from three o'clock one afternoon until eight the next morning. And the only tickets that were still available for us to buy were the front row seats. No wonder why! We snuggled the kids down for the night on the seats behind the driver and behind us, while we took the front view. All night long, while the rest of the bus was sawing wood, we were watching and wondering if we would ever see Mexico City.

The countryside and the mountains were beautiful, and the sight of all the different groups along the way made us realize all the more that all these groups were people for whom Christ died, and that all deserved to have the Word of God in a language they best understand. Also along the way, we saw little white crosses, scattered at different intervals, showing the places where people had lost there lives on the highway. And the speed and ferociousness with which the driver was taking those hair pin mountain turns, we had our own fears.

We committed our family to God. We had, of course, committed our own lives in dedication to Christ and for His service. And our children we had each dedicated to Christ when they were infants. But now, we prayed fervently, "Lord, we are all Yours and belong to You for Your purposes, times and plans. If this is to be our time to come to Yourself, let it be so, for each one of us has known You as our Savior and we are not afraid to die. We again commit ourselves to You and place our future in Your hands." We didn't sleep that entire night, staying awake in prayer.

The other bus trip was again on a mountain road. We had already travelled by bus up into the mountains in the Philippines where there was a lovely recreation area and were very impressed with the courtesy of the bus drivers on those roads. The steep and sharp curves required a wide turning radius and the drivers going down the mountain would yield when they could see the upcoming busses. They would find a way ahead of time to get out of the way. We saw this over and over and were so impressed.

Another time we were travelling in a two bus caravan from Manila to six hours further north of the well travelled roads. Our entire family was on our way to a New Testament dedication for the Kankanaey people. The bus drivers were not wild and crazy. That wasn't the problem. The problem was that the summer before there had been a major earthquake that had rocked those mountains. Whole villages fell off the face of the earth. Nobody could tell how many people there were, they just disappeared under the load of rock and dirt. The mountain roads were in various degrees of repair. The scariest times were the areas they called the saddlebacks. The road had disappeared in many places and they had pulled up a mound of rock and dirt, enough to drive across for the road to continue. Each time we crossed over one, we marveled at the skill and bravery of the driver, for many times, some of the wheels were barely on the road. The makeshift road was not quite as wide as a bus. It was a tense and nerve wracking time for us, but here we are, alive to tell about it. Many times we have SEEN God's hand of protection in our lives. How many times have we not even had a glimpse of His undergirding hand? Many untold, I'm sure.

I Thought I Said

It's long been said, "I know you think you understand what you thought you heard me say but I'm not sure you realize that what you thought you heard me say is not what I meant.

Communicate, communicate, communicate. It is so common to miss each other. The integrity of Christian harmony can sometimes be attributed to taking the time to make sure we mean the same things by our words as we listen with caring until understanding takes place. Often we divide unnecessarily because we misunderstand each other. And for whatever reason we are "too busy" to talk things out. That only builds walls of misunderstanding, division and hurts. It's hard to stay connected when we think we see things differently and divide over things that we just don't understand or even misinterpret. When I have taken the time to talk and listen until understanding takes place, even if we don't agree, we find a better sense of love and understanding. Then we can believe the best about each other, where we're committed to communicating through to understanding.

"Behold how good and pleasant it is when brothers live together in harmony. For there the Lord bestows His blessings, even life forevermore." Ps 133:1&3

"The thief comes to rob, kill and destroy, but I have come that you might have life abundantly."

Ganglion Cyst

Two of our translators arrived in Manila and I drove them to the doctors' office. Since it was a surgeon we were going to I got to thinking that I might have him check the lump on my wrist.

The Doctor called it a ganglion cyst, nothing serious, but if it bothered me he could remove it the following day. I went into Out Patient care at the hospital, again accompanied by the translators who would be having their procedures done also.

While I was in the doctors' office I noticed that he was rather jittery and looked nervous and his hands were even shaking. But I decided to trust his reputation. The next morning the removal of the cyst went well. It took only about twenty minutes and I was able to watch the whole procedure. My wrist was cut open and I could see the veins and muscles, how they connect and intertwine. I could see my main artery in the middle of it all. As a child I remembered my brother, Tom, after bashing his arm through glass had once had to have stitches. I recall them said something like, "fortunately he didn't cut the artery." I had this belief, no artery, no more use of hand.

So, laying there watching the doctor still working around inside my wrist and seeing my artery exposed, I prayed, "Lord, please don't let him cut the artery." It seemed to take him so long to finish in there, for he had long ago said that he had the ganglion out. All of a sudden, I looked over, and watched as he accidentally snipped, one quick accidental slip, and my artery was severed. Blood was spurting like a fountain, covering the doctor and his assistant.

I couldn't believe what I was seeing. God, didn't You just hear my earnest prayer? You knew I was afraid of this and now it's happened. Don't You care? Don't You love me? I couldn't believe this was now happening to me. I was scared and terribly disappointed with God.

But I did have an immediate answer to that nagging question. Yes, God does care and He was right there with me. I know He allows these kinds of trials ultimately for our good, could I trust Him? "Ok, Lord, I do trust You. I do hurt, though, and I'm scared and I'm not sure I'm ready to make the sacrifice You're asking of me. You know, Lord, that I'm a missionary and that requires me to do lots of writing to journal and to correspond with many people who make up our team and want to know what You're doing through our lives. And of course, this has to be my right hand, my writing hand. Well, Lord, my right hand belongs to You, for You to use or not to use at Your will. If I never write again, that is Yours to decide. I give it up. I know You love me, You have shown me in so many ways, how can I doubt Your love now when the trials come. To whom can I trust to be my Lord but You. I stand firm in my love for You and Your loving plan."

This wasn't an easy thing to say as the whole while, for the next one and a half hours, the doctor kept saying to his assistant, "I just can't seem to get it." There he was trying to reconnect my artery, and he kept repeating those dreadful words, "I just can't seem to get it."

I was in a meditative state, not thinking clearly, nor do I think I would have had the courage anyway to suggest to the doctor that he call for some help from another surgeon. Later I would think of that! In a shame culture such as the Philippines one in a high position such as a doctor, would never admit to being unable to do something; that would be too shameful. All I could do was to pray that the Lord would give me patience and strength to make it through this.

I was flipping back and forth between the thoughts toward the doctor, just hurry up and sew me together, I want to get out of here and the dis- appointment thoughts towards God, how come You didn't answer my prayer?" I was struggling with, why bother to pray? Although, I know God answers so marvelously sometimes in prayers we only barely think, and whew, there's the answer. And only He knows the countless times He answers heart cries we don't even think or express. But still my struggle was, why bother to pray if He lets the calamity happen anyway.

I finally came to the conclusion that prayer wasn't after all, bossing God around, being the lord ourselves. He says to let our requests be known to Him and He will give His peace. Not necessarily the answer my way. After a few weeks of struggling with this, I finally concluded that since God is sovereign, and I didn't doubt that at all, that He must be able to show me His love in a greater way by disappointing me this time than by answering me. Surely to know that He is Lord is more important to this pot of clay.

I walked out of the operating room much later than was expected by my frantic colleagues, who had been praying for me the whole time. Dave, who they had called as this progressed was just then arriving, so I was surrounded by their caring love. But the greatest joy was when I made the attempt at closing my fingers and opening them up. I leaped for joy, praising God that I could use my hand again, now all the more consecrated to His use.

The doctor has since retired, realizing that his surgery days are behind him. The only way to settle the injustice was to forgive the doctor and give him grace. We all blow it and have been forgiven much. I'm thankful to have my life, health, family, blessings of fellowship with the Lord, dear sisters and brothers,......

The Knife

The second Christmas we were in the Philippines we decided to go up to our translation center in the north for Christmas vacation. It's such a good place for our kids to play. Our friends up there were special and Dave and I could play tennis.

Before we left, one of our helpers asked if I'd mind if she climbed the coconut tree to pick the fruit. That was fine with me. She was a fairly new helper to us. After we were well on our way, it occurred to me that we don't own a machete. Oh, no, how will she open those coconuts? She wouldn't use my good expensive butcher knife from my kitchen, would she? I felt sick, but there was nothing to do now but hope she would not. This is typical of life as a household manager. Much of running a household I had always just done. I didn't think of telling someone else all the little details we have learned over the years. And culturally how we do things is often very different and we all learn the hard way.

When we returned, I barely said hello before I ran to the kitchen drawer to check out the knife. It now was wavy top to bottom. I was just sick, yet it was my responsibility to teach her. I did feel the loss because the knives had been a gift from Dave our first Christmas. Oh, well, another THING that can't matter in light of eternity.

Pets in His Service

There is always so much to learn about life, even of God's character through experiences with our pets.

The first time I remember praying about a pet problem was with a cat. For a short while we had a cat. And when it was new to us, I remember letting it outdoors that first night. Not ever having a cat before, I didn't know anything about their behavior. It was out a few hours, and then I started to worry, I didn't know if they find their way home in a strange new place. It was our daughter's bedtime and her cat hadn't returned yet. We thought it was a goner. I prayed and thought I'd call for it one more time before going to bed. And there, much to my surprise, Diamond came walking up the back walk. Thank you, Lord.

Diamond didn't stay with us long, for I soon discovered that I was terribly allergic to cats. I always thought that people who didn't like cats used the allergy excuse to not have to put up with them. But I found out differently.

Our next significant pet was once we were in the Philippines. The first three months we were there, we stayed at another missionaries home while they took a short furlough. That gave us three months in their home to be looking for a place of our own. The house came with a van, a house girl, a dog and a hamster. The dog was a big Doberman.

One night the children had had the hamster out playing in the house. Then they forgot about it. Unfortunately, the house also had a sliding screen door to the big yard. I happened to glance at the cage, and said, "Where's the hamster?" We all went on a hamster hunt, nothing new. Usually we found him cuddled up next to the sofa leg, but not tonight. Then we saw that the door was a bit ajar, enough for the little hamster to fit through. Since it was dark we knew we could never see it in the big yard. We thought that that was one less pet that these folks would be coming back to.

A short while later the dog came to the door. Once we let him in we noticed right away that he had the hamster in his mouth. We told him to drop it, expecting quite a mutilated rodent. To our surprise, here was this slimy but very much alive hamster. The dog had known that the little guy didn't belong out there in the big bad world, had rescued him and brought him safely home. Well, we all turned it into a smothering time and were so thankful for how God cares about even the little things we face.

After we were settled into own home, we started to get all kinds of pets. We raised baby chicks that turned into big, messy chickens. And we had rabbits, turtles, hamsters, guinea pigs and dogs. One day just after the kids had left for school we noticed that one of the guinea pigs had gotten his hand stuck in the cage and it appeared that all night he was unable to get to his water, so he died.

When the kids returned from school we broke the news to them that the guinea pig they loved had died. This guinea pig was Snicker, the survivor was Doodle. When Ben heard the news, he said, "Well, at least it wasn't Fluffy, his dog." They dug a hole and made a big ceremony of burying the guinea pig. Then Randall and Paul left on their bikes to go around the block with the two dogs following behind. Quite soon afterwards, Randall came home screaming that a dog had been hit on the next block. Dave raced off on foot following Randall, while I got the car and caught up with them. In Manila, the neighborhood we lived in, most of the houses have big high fences around them to protect from thieves.

On the next block, the boys were just passing by a house, and they went by a gate that had been left open by a maid. Out from the yard leaped three huge German Shepherds dogs right at our boys on their bikes. Fortunately the boys kept their heads. One of the dogs was so frightened by them that he jumped out into the street right into the path of an oncoming truck. He hobbled to the side of the road and lay there panting. Paul was so frightened that the big dogs were going to attack our dog,that he stood by him to protect him while Randall ran home to get help. We all watched as Fluffy gave up the fight. We placed him in the back of the van and headed for home. That was such a shock, yet the reality of how close we had come to loosing one of the boys was even more shocking to us.

The children cried and cried, and we encouraged them to let all their feelings come out. Before the night was over, we had forgiven the people who left the gate open and had the dogs who did such damage. We also told God that we trust that He has a loving purpose for everything that happens to us so we trust Him. We all prayed together that God would comfort us in our loss, and that He would use it for His glory.

We had friends coming for dinner, and as this happened right at supper time, we had anticipated that we weren't going to be in the mood for company, that we would ask them if we might make a rain check with them. But our company was late, so that by the time they arrived we had gotten through a bit of the shock and pain and were ready for them. It turned out that their children, being just a bit older than ours were uniquely able to minister to the needs and feelings of our kids. They had also experienced the loss of a dog. So we all joined together for a second burial of the day.

Three weeks later, I was standing on the street corner with Valerie, Ben and the guinea pig on our way to school where Doodle was to appear as show and tell at preschool. We had only one car I was waiting for a taxi. We often use other public transportation such as jeepneys or tricycles as our second vehicle but since we had a cage I opted for a taxi this time. A blue Volkswagen bug pulled up to the curb. The man inside asked me if I'd like a ride. My first thought was what my mother had said probably thirty years earlier, "don't get into a car with strangers." Everybody knows that, right? But here was this very old man, and kind, inviting the whole lot of us in. It was such a surprise and I had the feeling that he was harmless. When I looked inside his car, I saw a little sticker on his dash, Jesus. I decided, why not, and we all hopped in. Val and Ben were excited, for they had been recently playing a game called slug bug, where the first person who sees a VW gets a point and somehow they keep track of who has how many points, and now they were riding in one.

I had a nice conversation with the man. I found that he also lived in the neighborhood with his daughters' family. Just before we headed down the hill a block from our mission headquarters where I was going, a peculiar question came out of my mouth. "Does your daughter happen to have three big dogs?" "Why yes, she does, how did you know?" Good grief, Lord, can this really be happening? I told him that we were the people whose dog had been hit out front of their house. He turned instantly sad and said that they had felt so bad, knowing that it had been somebody's pet. They were so sorry. I was able to tell him that we had forgiven them. We got to the office, and got out and never saw him again.

We wondered whether that was God's loving purpose for allowing it to happen. That this man could know the forgiveness that comes from God. We talked about it that if God had used our Fluffy for this man to feel a touch of God's love, than the loss was worth it.

Piano

When we were first called to the mission field, the thought of giving up our worldly possessions was not difficult. We wanted to be free to go wherever God was leading us and we knew that a house full of stuff would get in the way. We had five huge garage sales to dispose of all the worldly accumulation of our first eleven years of marriage. It was so freeing, it felt like a good bath. Keeping all that stuff has its own weight. Having to keep it all clean, working, insured, protected from robbers and repaired. We now were down to just what we really used and some things that have sentimental value. It's a wonderful clean feeling.

But I did have a question for God. What about my piano? Is it possible to bring it with me? I was picturing how a young child pulls along a toy on a string. I had prayed long and hard in want of a piano, claiming God's promise in the Psalms that "no good thing would the Lord withhold from them that walk blamelessly?" Was I not His and committed to follow Him? Yes. That made me blameless. And wasn't music in the home for a family a good thing? Again, yes. So I knew it was just a matter of time before He would allow me my hearts desire for a piano. And six months before we were called to the mission field I received an inheritance from my dear great aunt, enabling me to buy a nice new piano. My husband and I enjoyed picking one out together. Now we were being asked to let it go.

In some ways that was not difficult. I committed it to God when I got it and I recognized that it was pure and simply a gift from Him. But it was hard to think of giving it up. We sold most of our furniture, but brought the piano with us to Dallas for the one and a half year training process that was required us before going overseas. The last two weeks at the piano, I cried often. The hymns were both a comfort and a reminder of truth. "A tent or a cottage, why should I care, they're building a palace for me over there." Owning earthly things had lost its hold in my life. But the piano, sigh Lord. "Anywhere with Jesus I can safely go, anywhere He leads me in this world below...."

Well, the good of this part is that our piano was to be used while we were away by some very dear friends who had been on the mission field many years and now were back and didn't own such a thing. She was thrilled to have a piano and received it as a gift from God to her.

The first day we were in the Philippines we received a call from another missionary who was leaving in a week for a three month furlough and they wanted to know if we would stay in their home while they were away. We decided that would be great and would give us three months of looking for a suitable home of our own. One week before they returned, we still had no place of our own. We had no idea that finding housing would be so difficult, but it was.

Finally, a note was passed to us in Sunday school about another missionary who was going on a one year leave who needed someone to house sit. Would we be willing? That was really hard for us. We wanted to get established in a place of our own but with time running out we decided to check it out and see if God was leading us there. Truth is we really didn't have enough money to set up our own home. We operated that first term on a shoestring budget.

We saw the house and it was really nice. We told them we'd pray about it and let them know the next day. We decided that even if it wasn't what we desired we felt it was what God would have us do. So we went back the next day to talk about details. The wife informed me as we walked by the piano that they had just gotten it three months earlier and that nobody in their home plays. She hoped that we'd get some enjoyment out of it.

In my bed that night, I nearly leaped for joy at the realization of what God had done. Three months earlier I was crying heartily at the pain of leaving my piano, and my beloved heavenly Father was at the same time preparing my new home in the

Philippines for me - with a Piano. Oh, marvelous love. How, could I ever doubt Your love or Your Sovereignty. Thank You, Lord, for the lesson.

When that family returned the following year and we moved into our own home, another missionary was leaving at that same time and asked if we'd like first look at their household of furniture. We did, and bought the whole batch, including his Piano! So now, I have not one piano, but one on each side of the ocean. Do I ever feel rich!!

W ell, that is it for now. There are many more stories in my file but I need to stop so this isn't overwhelmingly long. I trust that you have seen something new about how much God loves you as you've read my story. He loves you as much as he loves me!!

Blessings to you, my fellow Pilgrim.

Breinigsville, PA USA
25 January 2011
254065BV00004BA/1/P